The Indian Gut Project

Fix your Gut Improve Digestion, Combat Bloating, Promote Weight Loss With Indian Probiotics Food

VINDHYA SINGH

Table of Contents

1
CHAPTER

2
CHAPTER
GUT HEALTH

3

CHAPTER

THE INDIAN PROBIOTIC RICH DIET

1
CHAPTER

Introduction

In the intricate landscape of human health, one area has gained significant attention and understanding in recent years: the gut and its diverse inhabitants, collectively known as the micro-biome. This microscopic universe, teeming with countless bacteria, viruses, fungi, and other microorganisms, plays a pivotal role in our overall well-being. The symbiotic relationship between these tiny inhabitants and our body is nothing short of fascinating, influencing everything from digestion and immunity to mental health and disease prevention. In this exploration of gut health and the micro-biome, we embark on a journey to unravel the mysteries within our own bodies. The human gut, often referred to as the "second brain," is a complex ecosystem where trillions of microorganisms reside, creating a delicate balance that is essential for our health. Recent scientific advancements have illuminated the profound impact this intricate microbial community has on our lives. From shaping our immune responses to affecting our mood and metabolism, the micro-biome is a key player in the intricate web of human biology.

The human gastrointestinal (GI) tract, covering a vast area of 250-400 m², acts as a crucial link between the human body, environmental elements, and antigens. Throughout a person's lifetime, around 60 tonnes of food journey through this complex network, carrying with them various microorganisms from the environment. This influx presents a substantial challenge to the integrity of the gut. The 'gut micro-biota,' consisting of bacteria, archaea, and eukarya in the GI tract, coevolves with humans, forming a vital relationship. With an estimated 10^14 microorganisms, this community, often called a 'superorganism,' influences gut integrity and immune regulation. Dysbiosis, or microbial imbalance, can disrupt these processes, impacting overall health and contributing to various diseases. Furthermore, we will investigate the profound connections between gut health and various diseases, ranging from common digestive disorders to autoimmune conditions. Understanding how the gut micro-biome influences the aging process and exploring the relationship between gut inflammation and disease will provide valuable insights into maintaining optimal health throughout life.

This book is not just a compilation of scientific knowledge; it is a guide to empower readers with practical information. We will unravel strategies to nurture and support our gut health, emphasizing the importance of mindful eating, probiotics, and other lifestyle choices that can positively impact our micro-biome. So, let us embark on this enlightening expedition into the depths of our own bodies, where trillions of microorganisms work tirelessly to shape our health and well-being.

VINDHYA SINGH

Importance Of Gut Health

The gut micro-biota is complex and challenging to characterize. Enterotypes have been proposed using metrics such as alpha species diversity, the ratio of Firmicutes to Bacteroidetes phyla, and the relative abundance of beneficial genera (e.g., *Bifidobacterium*, *Akkermansia*) versus facultative anaerobes (*E. coli*), pro-inflammatory *Ruminococcus*, or nonbacterial microbes. Micro-biota composition and relative populations of bacterial species are linked to physiologic health along different axes. Maintaining gut health is vital because it influences various aspects of our overall well-being. The gut micro-biome, comprising trillions of microorganisms residing in the digestive tract, plays a crucial role in human health. Scientific research has provided substantial evidence supporting its importance:

1. Digestion and Nutrient Absorption: Gut bacteria assist in breaking down complex carbohydrates and fibers that human digestive enzymes can't process. This breakdown results in the production of short-chain fatty acids (SCFAs) that provide an energy source for the body and support nutrient absorption.	**2. Immune System Regulation:** The gut micro-biome regulates the immune system, influencing the development and functioning of immune cells. Studies have shown that a diverse and balanced micro-biome helps prevent autoimmune diseases and allergies by modulating immune responses.
3. Mental Health: Emerging research suggests a strong connection between the gut and brain, known as the gut-brain axis. The micro-biome produces neurotransmitters like serotonin, impacting mood and mental health. Imbalances in the gut micro-biota have been linked to conditions such as anxiety, depression, and even neurodegenerative diseases.	**4. Metabolism and Obesity:** Certain gut bacteria influence metabolism, affecting how the body stores fat, regulates blood sugar, and responds to hormones that control hunger and fullness. Disruptions in the micro-biome composition have been associated with obesity and metabolic disorders.
5. Protection against Pathogens: Beneficial bacteria in the gut provide a protective barrier against harmful pathogens. They outcompete harmful microbes for resources and produce antimicrobial substances, preventing infections. Probiotics, live beneficial bacteria, have been used to treat various gastrointestinal infections.	**6. Inflammatory Bowel Diseases (IBD):** Studies have identified alterations in the gut micro-biota composition in individuals with IBD, including Crohn's disease and ulcerative colitis. Restoring a healthy balance through fecal micro-biota transplantation (FMT) has shown promising results in managing these conditions.

7. Cancer Prevention: Certain gut bacteria are involved in metabolizing dietary compounds into anti-cancer substances. Additionally, a balanced gut micro-biome strengthens the immune system, aiding in the detection and elimination of cancerous cells.	**8. Response to Cancer Immunotherapy:** Recent studies have indicated that the composition of the gut micro-biota influences the effectiveness of cancer immunotherapies. Specific bacteria have been associated with enhanced responses to immunotherapy treatments.
9. Longevity: Research in animal models suggests that manipulating the gut micro-biome can extend lifespan. Although this area is still being explored, it opens avenues for understanding the role of the micro-biome in aging processes.	**10. Communication center:** The gut micro-biota communicates with various organs and systems in the body, influencing their functions. This communication network, known as the gut-brain axis, plays a vital role in regulating metabolism, hormones, and even immune responses, ensuring the body operates harmoniously.

In summary, the gut micro-biome's significance in human health is supported by a wealth of scientific evidence, highlighting its impact on digestion, immunity, mental health, metabolism, and disease prevention. Ongoing research continues to uncover new connections and therapeutic possibilities related to the gut micro-biota.

The Science Of Gut Micro-Biome

The composition of the human gut micro-biota undergoes significant changes in early life, influenced by factors such as delivery mode, feeding methods, and antibiotic use. These factors affect microbial diversity and community assembly. Stochastic ecological processes, including random events like antibiotic treatments, play a substantial role in shaping the micro-biome, accounting for unexplained variation. Early-life events impact the gut micro-biota composition, potentially influencing the risk of immune-mediated diseases. In healthy adults, the gut micro-biome is stable and shaped more by environmental factors than genetics. Micro-biota diversity is associated with health, while factors like sedentary lifestyle and unhealthy diets deplete the micro-biome, increasing chronic disease risks. Dietary changes and medical interventions, including antibiotics, lead to micro-biome alterations. Microbial diversity correlates with stool consistency and transit times, influencing metabolism. The micro-biome shows resilience after mild perturbations but may suffer incomplete repair after severe disruptions. Dysbiosis, or micro-biome alteration, is common in various diseases.

The science of gut micro-biome deals with studying the gut micro-biome and unraveling it's complexity of this microbial world. The science of the gut micro-biome delves into the intricate relationships between diverse microorganisms residing in the gut and their profound impact on human health. Understanding these interactions not only sheds light on the complexity of our biological systems but also holds the key to developing innovative treatments and interventions for various health conditions.

1. **Diversity and Composition:** The gut micro-biota is incredibly diverse, with thousands of different species. Each person's micro-biome is unique, influenced by factors like genetics, diet, environment, and early life experiences. Researchers employ advanced DNA sequencing techniques to identify and categorize these diverse microbial communities.	2. **Factors Influencing Composition:** Various factors shape the composition of the gut micro-biome. This includes birth methods (vaginal delivery vs. Cesarean section), breastfeeding vs. formula feeding, antibiotic usage, and dietary habits. Understanding how these factors impact the microbial composition provides valuable insights into the development of a healthy micro-biome.

The gut micro-biota interacts with various functions of the human body such as

1. **Digestive Functions**: One of the primary roles of the gut micro-biota is aiding in digestion. These microbes help break down complex carbohydrates and fibers that human enzymes cannot digest, producing essential nutrients and short-chain fatty acids in the process. This assists in nutrient absorption and energy production.	2. **Immune System Regulation:** The gut micro-biota plays a crucial role in training the immune system. Beneficial microbes help educate immune cells, ensuring they respond appropriately to harmful invaders while tolerating harmless substances. This interaction is vital for a well-balanced and responsive immune system.
3. **Metabolic Impact:** Gut microbes influence metabolism by modulating energy storage and expenditure. Imbalances in the micro-biome composition have been linked to metabolic disorders such as obesity and diabetes. Certain microbes can affect the body's utilization of nutrients, impacting overall metabolic health.	4. **Neurological Connections:** The gut-brain axis represents the bidirectional communication between the gut and the brain. Recent research has revealed that the gut micro-biota can influence brain function and behavior. Microbes in the gut produce neurotransmitters and interact with neural pathways, potentially impacting mental health and conditions like depression and anxiety.

5. **Disease Prevention and Defense:** A healthy gut micro-biome serves as a protective shield, keeping harmful pathogens away. Beneficial microbes create antimicrobial substances, overpowering harmful bacteria, and defending the body against infections and diseases.

Regional Diversity In India

The colonization of the gut by microbes starts at birth, influenced by factors like age, diet, genetics, gender, location, and health. Studying diverse human subjects is vital for understanding the gut micro-biome. In India, diverse genetic backgrounds, diets, and geography create challenges and opportunities. While global studies link the gut micro-biome to diseases like obesity, detailed analysis of these links in the Indian population is lacking. Research involving Indians can shed unique light on micro-biome associations with various factors and diseases, distinct from Western studies. This review explores the gut micro-biome's significance for human health, highlighting the current status of research in the Indian context. In the past, diseases like obesity and diabetes were less common in India due to different lifestyles. However, recent socio-economic changes have made Indians more susceptible to metabolic diseases such as coronary heart disease, diabetes, and obesity. India also struggles with malnourishment. These shifts in health issues are linked to alterations in the gut micro-biome, impacting the host's well-being. India, with its diverse population and rich cultural heritage, exhibits unique aspects of gut health that have piqued the interest of researchers worldwide. The study of gut health in India reveals a multifaceted landscape shaped by genetic diversity, regional variations, cultural practices, and dietary choices. Research articles from diverse fields continue to unravel the unique aspects of the Indian gut micro-biota, providing valuable insights into the interplay between culture, diet, and gut health in this diverse and vibrant nation.

Genetic diversity in India influences distinct gut micro-biota patterns, with studies revealing significant variations among different Indian communities. Additionally, regional disparities in gut micro-biome composition are linked to factors like climate and altitude. Furthermore, research indicates a correlation between gut micro-biota alterations and diseases like irritable bowel syndrome (IBS) and inflammatory bowel diseases (IBD) in India, reflecting the nation's unique health challenges. Regarding cultural and dietary influences, India's diverse dietary habits, ranging from vegetarian to non-vegetarian diets, result in significant differences in gut micro-biota composition. Vegetarians and non-vegetarians exhibit distinct microbial profiles. Traditional fermented foods like idli and dosa contribute to a healthy gut, as studies emphasize their probiotic potential. Moreover, Indian spices and herbs such as turmeric and cumin impact gut micro-biota composition, promoting gut health. Understanding these factors provides valuable insights into personalized nutrition and health outcomes in the Indian population.

VINDHYA SINGH

1. Genetic Diversity:

Genetic diversity plays a fundamental role in shaping the gut micro-biota composition within populations. In the context of India, this diversity is exceptionally pronounced due to the country's complex history of migration, intermixing of various ethnic groups, and diverse cultural practices. This genetic variation is not only evident in the physical traits and genetic markers of the population but also extends to the intricate world of gut micro-biota. Several research studies, including a comprehensive have meticulously investigated the genetic influence on gut micro-biome variations among different Indian communities. The findings from these studies reveal that specific genetic factors are correlated with distinct patterns in the gut micro-biota composition. Certain genetic markers or variations in the human genome can influence the types and abundance of microorganisms that inhabit the gastrointestinal tract. Understanding the genetic underpinnings of gut micro-biota variation not only sheds light on the evolutionary history of populations but also provides insights into the potential links between genetic factors, gut health, and susceptibility to certain diseases. This knowledge is invaluable for personalized medicine approaches, as it allows for tailored interventions based on an individual's genetic predispositions, ultimately leading to more effective treatments and improved health outcomes. India's population displays remarkable genetic diversity, leading to distinct patterns in the gut micro-biota composition.

2. Geographical Variations:

The gut micro-biome, the diverse community of microorganisms residing in the human intestines, exhibits unique compositions based on geographic locations. In India, this diversity is particularly striking, with significant regional disparities observed. Research studies have delved into these geographical variations, providing crucial insights into the factors shaping India's diverse gut micro-biota landscape. The factors contributing to regional disparities are

a. Climate: India boasts a wide range of climates, from the humid regions along the coasts to the arid landscapes of its deserts. Climate affects not only the availability of certain food resources but also the types of bacteria and other microorganisms that thrive in these environments. As a result, people living in different climatic zones develop unique gut micro-biota compositions tailored to their local climates.	**b. Altitude:** India's diverse topography includes plains, plateaus, and the towering Himalayan Mountains. Altitude impacts factors such as oxygen levels and atmospheric pressure, which, in turn, influence the gut micro-biota. Microbial communities adapt to varying oxygen concentrations, leading to distinct gut micro-biome profiles among populations residing at different altitudes.

> **c. Local Environment:** Urban areas with high pollution levels, agricultural regions with pesticide exposure, and rural communities with different agricultural practices all contribute to the local environment's impact on the gut micro-biota. Additionally, access to clean water, sanitation, and hygiene practices significantly influences the gut micro-biome's diversity, especially in more remote or underdeveloped regions.

Several other studies have shed light on these regional variations, emphasizing the intricate interplay between environmental factors and the gut micro-biome. By understanding how climate, altitude, and local environment shape gut micro-biota diversity, scientists can uncover potential links to various health outcomes. These findings have significant implications for public health initiatives, especially in India, where diverse gut micro-biota profiles might contribute to varying disease susceptibilities. Tailored interventions considering regional disparities can be developed to promote gut health, prevent diseases, and enhance overall well-being. Moreover, this research underscores the importance of considering geographical variations in micro-biome-related studies, emphasizing the need for targeted, region-specific approaches in the field of gut micro-biota research.

3. Disease Susceptibility:

India faces unique health challenges, including a high prevalence of gastrointestinal diseases. Researchers, exemplified the intricate relationship between gut micro-biota alterations and specific diseases, notably irritable bowel syndrome (IBS) and inflammatory bowel diseases (IBD) within the Indian population.

a. Irritable Bowel Syndrome (IBS): IBS is a prevalent gastrointestinal disorder characterized by abdominal pain, discomfort, and altered bowel habits. Studies in India, including the one cited, have delved into how disruptions in the gut micro-biota composition might contribute to IBS. Variations in microbial diversity, imbalance in beneficial and harmful bacteria, and altered microbial metabolites are among the factors investigated.	**b. Inflammatory Bowel Diseases (IBD):** IBD, comprising conditions like Crohn's disease and ulcerative colitis, involves chronic inflammation of the gastrointestinal tract. Researchers have explored the gut micro-biota's role in triggering and perpetuating inflammation in the intestines. Changes in the gut microbial community structure, immune responses to specific bacteria, and the influence of genetic factors are areas of intensive study.

> **c. Unique Challenges in India:** India's unique health landscape, encompassing diverse dietary habits, genetic predispositions, and environmental factors, adds complexity to understanding disease susceptibility. The prevalence of specific diseases in the Indian population might be influenced by culturally rooted dietary practices, regional variations in gut micro-biota, and lifestyle factors like stress and hygiene standards.

Understanding the correlation between gut micro-biota alterations and diseases like IBS and IBD is pivotal for developing targeted therapeutic interventions. Tailored treatments considering the unique genetic, dietary, and environmental factors in the Indian context can potentially alleviate disease burden. Moreover, ongoing research in this area holds the promise of unveiling novel biomarkers, probiotic therapies, and personalized approaches to manage and prevent gastrointestinal diseases, thereby significantly improving the quality of life for affected individuals in India and beyond.

Cultural and dietary factors significantly shape the gut micro-biota, playing a pivotal role in human health. Diverse dietary habits and cultural practices influence the composition and functionality of the gut microbes. Understanding these influences provides valuable insights into personalized nutrition and health outcomes.

a. Vegetarian vs. Non-Vegetarian Diets: India's dietary landscape spans from predominantly vegetarian to non-vegetarian practices. Comprehensive studies have meticulously compared the gut micro-biota of vegetarians and non-vegetarians. These studies have illuminated significant disparities attributable to the consumption of plant-based or animal-based diets. Vegetarians, relying primarily on plant-derived foods, exhibit a gut micro-biota rich in fiber-digesting bacteria, emphasizing the impact of diet on microbial composition. In contrast, non-vegetarians, incorporating animal proteins, showcase a micro-biota profile influenced by animal-derived nutrients. These findings underscore the pivotal role of dietary choices in shaping the gut micro-biome and offer valuable insights into the health implications associated with diverse diets in India.

b. Fermented Foods: Fermented foods are integral to Indian culinary traditions and have been linked to gut health benefits. Research's has delved into the impact of traditional fermented foods like idli and dosa on the gut micro-biota. Fermented foods, rich in probiotic bacteria, enhance gut microbial diversity and contribute to a balanced gut ecosystem. The presence of beneficial bacteria in these foods, such as lactobacilli and bifidobacteria, fortifies the gut's defense mechanisms, aiding digestion and promoting overall intestinal health. This research underscores the significance of fermented foods as natural probiotics, emphasizing their role in maintaining a healthy gut micro-biome in the Indian population.

c. Spices and Herbs: Indian cuisine is renowned for its vibrant array of spices and herbs, not only for their culinary appeal but also for their medicinal properties. Studies, exemplified by research have delved into the influence of spices like turmeric and cumin on gut micro-biota composition. These spices, abundant in bioactive compounds, exhibit antimicrobial and anti inflammatory properties. Incorporating spices into the diet modulates the gut micro-biota, promoting the growth of beneficial bacteria while inhibiting harmful pathogens. Turmeric, in particular, contains curcumin, known for its antioxidant and anti-inflammatory effects on the gut. Such research highlights the potential of Indian spices and herbs in shaping a balanced gut micro-biome, offering not just culinary delights but also significant health benefits to those enjoying the diverse flavors of Indian cuisine.

Good Bugs And Bad One In The Gut

The human gut is a complex ecosystem hosting trillions of microorganisms, collectively known as the gut micro-biota. Among these microbes, there are both beneficial and harmful species, each playing a vital role in maintaining gut health.

1.   Beneficial Microbes:

a. *Lactobacillus* **and** *Bifidobacterium*: These probiotic bacteria are fundamental for digestion. They break down complex carbohydrates, lactose, and fiber, aiding in nutrient absorption. *Lactobacillus* and *Bifidobacterium* also promote a balanced gut environment by inhibiting the growth of harmful bacteria.	**b.** *Firmicutes* **and** *Bacteroidetes*: These phyla are crucial for breaking down dietary fibers and complex carbohydrates into short-chain fatty acids (SCFAs) such as butyrate. SCFAs serve as an energy source for intestinal cells and help maintain the integrity of the gut lining.
c. Short-Chain Fatty Acid Producers: Certain microbes, like *Faecalibacterium prausnitzii*, produce SCFAs that play a vital role in immune regulation and anti-inflammatory responses. SCFAs are essential for the overall health of the gut and the entire body.	

2.   Harmful Microbes:

a. *Escherichia coli* **(E. coli):** While some strains are harmless, pathogenic *E. coli* can cause severe foodborne illnesses and gastrointestinal issues. They produce toxins that damage the intestinal lining.	**b.** *Salmonella*: *Salmonella* bacteria are responsible for food poisoning, leading to symptoms like diarrhea, fever, and abdominal cramps. They invade the gut lining, causing inflammation and disrupting normal gut function.
c. *Clostridium difficile:* *C. difficile* overgrowth disrupts the balance of the gut micro-biota, leading to infections and symptoms ranging from mild diarrhea to severe colitis. Antibiotic use often triggers *C. difficile* infections.	**d.** *Helicobacter pylori:* This bacterium infects the stomach lining, causing ulcers and increasing the risk of gastric cancers. It weakens the stomach's protective mucus layer, leading to inflammation and damage.
e. *Campylobacter jejuni:* *Campylobacter* bacteria cause gastroenteritis, leading to symptoms such as diarrhea, abdominal pain, and fever. In severe cases, it can lead to dehydration and hospitalization.	

Maintaining the balance

Harmonious balances between beneficial and harmful microbes are vital for gut health. Disruptions in this balance, often caused by factors like poor diet, stress, antibiotics, and infections, can lead to dysbiosis- a condition associated with various gastrointestinal disorders, autoimmune diseases, and even mental health issues. Maintaining this equilibrium requires a diverse and fiber-rich diet, regular exercise, hydration, and, in some cases, probiotic supplementation. Understanding the delicate interplay between these microbes is crucial for overall well-being, emphasizing the importance of nurturing a healthy gut micro-biota for a healthier life.

Microbial effects on aging

The intricate relationship between the human micro-biota and aging has become a focal point of scientific exploration. Within the human body the micro-biota, significantly influence the aging process. Research indicates that these microbes play vital roles in immune function, metabolism, and neurological health as individuals age. Understanding this dynamic interplay offers insights into strategies for promoting healthier aging and improving overall well-being.

a. Immune Function: The gut micro-biota significantly impacts the immune system, and alterations in its composition are associated with age-related immune dysregulation. A balanced gut micro-biota helps in maintaining a robust immune response, crucial for warding off infections and diseases in older adults.	**b. Metabolism:** Changes in the gut micro-biota composition have been linked to metabolic disorders prevalent in aging, such as diabetes and obesity. Certain microbes aid in the breakdown of dietary components and regulate energy metabolism, affecting weight management and overall metabolic health.
c. Neurological Health: Emerging research indicates a strong gut-brain connection. Imbalances in the gut micro-biota have been linked to neurological conditions like Alzheimer's disease and Parkinson's disease. The micro-biota influences the central nervous system, potentially impacting cognitive function and age-related neurodegeneration.	

Strategies for Maintaining Healthy Gut Micro-biota in Older Age

a. Dietary Modifications: Consuming a diverse and fiber-rich diet supports a healthy gut micro-biota. High-fiber foods, such as fruits, vegetables, whole grains, and legumes, provide nourishment for beneficial microbes, promoting their growth and diversity.	**b. Probiotic and Prebiotic Supplements:** Probiotics are live beneficial bacteria, and prebiotics are substances that promote the growth of beneficial microbes. Incorporating probiotic-rich foods like yogurt and fermented products, along with prebiotic sources like garlic and onions, can enhance gut health.

c. Regular Exercise: Physical activity is linked to a more diverse gut micro-biota. Exercise promotes microbial diversity and a balanced microbial community, contributing to overall health and well-being in older age.	**d. Reducing Stress:** Chronic stress can adversely affect the gut micro-biota composition. Stress management techniques such as meditation, yoga, and relaxation exercises can positively impact the gut-brain axis, maintaining a healthier gut micro-biota.

Understanding and harnessing the power of the gut micro-biota in the aging process holds the promise of improving the quality of life for older adults. By employing strategies that support a healthy gut micro-biota, individuals can potentially mitigate age-related health issues and promote overall well-being as they age.

Gut Inflammation And Permeability

The gastrointestinal epithelium serves as a crucial barrier, allowing nutrient absorption while preventing harmful substances from entering the body. Tight junctions (TJs) between cells play a pivotal role in maintaining this barrier. The claudin family of proteins primarily forms TJs, and their dysregulation has been linked to mucosal inflammation, as seen in conditions like Inflammatory Bowel Disease (IBD). While studies in mice manipulating TJ proteins have yielded varied results, indicating their multifaceted roles, it is clear that these proteins not only regulate permeability but also influence immune responses and tissue repair. This review provides insights into the intricate mechanisms of mucosal inflammation, emphasizing the complex nature of these disease processes. Chronic gut inflammation, an intricate interplay of immune responses and genetic factors, has far-reaching implications. In-depth studies illuminate the underlying immunological dysregulation in chronic gut inflammation, elucidating pathways that contribute to conditions like Crohn's disease. This chronic inflammation extends its influence systemically, as evidenced by research linking gastrointestinal inflammation with cardiovascular diseases. Understanding the molecular and genetic underpinnings of chronic inflammation is pivotal, enabling targeted therapeutic strategies that not only mitigate local gut disorders but also curb its systemic impact, enhancing overall health.

Importance of Gut Barrier Function and Its Maintenance

The gut barrier fortified by tight junction and mucosal defense acts as the body's frontline defense. Comprehensive studies, exemplified the complexities of gut barrier function, emphasizing its vital role in preventing harmful substances from entering the bloodstream. Several studies underscore the link between a compromised gut barrier and autoimmune diseases, shedding light on the profound implications of a permeable gut. Interventions targeting gut barrier maintenance, such as specialized dietary approaches, personalized probiotic regimens, and stress management techniques, serve as key tools. These interventions bolster the gut lining, ensuring it remains resilient against inflammation-induced permeability, thereby safeguarding overall health and fostering a balanced immune response. By delving deeper into the intricate dynamics of gut inflammation and barrier function, researchers and healthcare practitioners gain nuanced insights. These insights empower the development of tailored therapeutic approaches, shaping a future where individuals can navigate the complexities of chronic inflammation with precision and foster enduring well-being.

VINDHYA SINGH

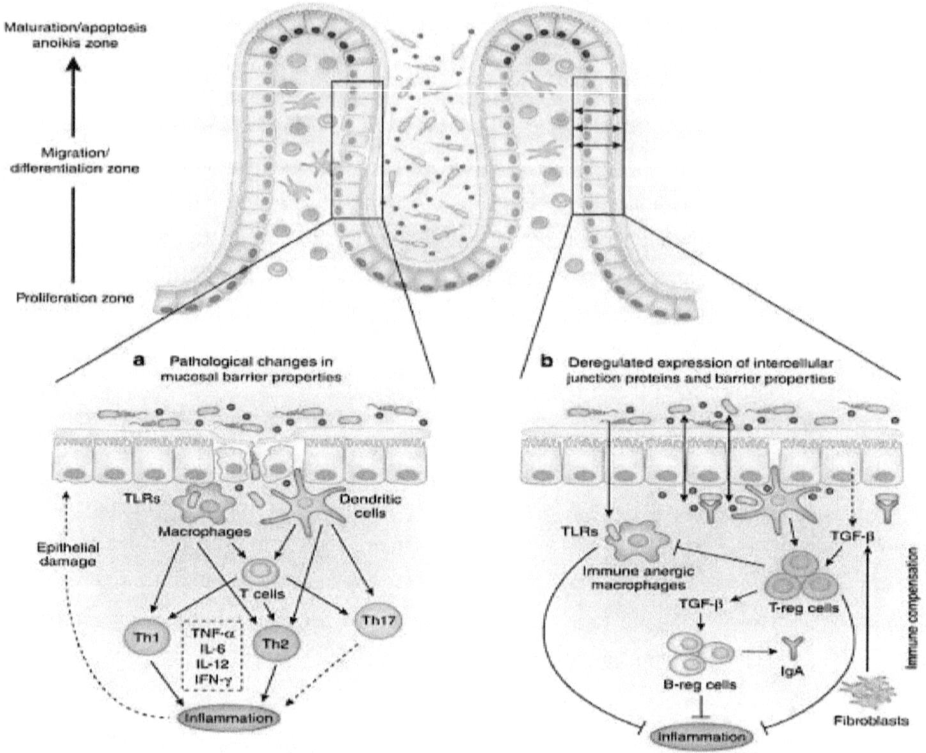

Figure 1 — The intestinal epithelium acts as a critical barrier, shielding the mucosal immune system from luminal antigens. (a) When this barrier is compromised, it triggers an overactive mucosal immune response, leading to chronic inflammation. (b) Interestingly, a leaky gut caused solely by tight junction openings might not directly cause inflammation; instead, it can stimulate an adaptive immune response due to heightened immune activity. The eventual impact may rely on non-junctional effects of proteins associated with the barrier, potentially modified during inflammatory conditions (*Ahmad et,al. 2017*).

Autoimmune Diseases And Leaky Gut: Unraveling The Connection

Autoimmune diseases, a diverse group of disorders where the immune system mistakenly attacks the body's own cells, have long puzzled researchers due to their complex origins. Recent investigations have shed light on a potential link between autoimmune diseases and a phenomenon known as "leaky gut." Leaky gut, scientifically referred to as increased intestinal permeability, occurs when the tight junctions between intestinal cells become compromised, allowing substances to leak into the bloodstream that would normally be blocked. This heightened permeability is hypothesized to trigger or exacerbate autoimmune responses, contributing to the development and progression of various autoimmune conditions.

The intestinal epithelium acts as the body's primary defense against external invaders. When the integrity of this barrier is compromised, it permits the entry of antigens, bacteria, and toxins into the bloodstream. This breach in the gut barrier may lead to the immune system mistakenly recognizing these substances as threats, triggering an autoimmune response against the body's own tissues. Several factors, including genetic predisposition, dietary factors, stress, and environmental triggers, can influence the development of leaky gut and contribute to the onset of autoimmune diseases Research has highlighted the intricate relationship between increased intestinal permeability and autoimmune diseases. Conditions like celiac disease, Crohn's disease, and rheumatoid arthritis have shown associations with leaky gut. In these disorders, compromised gut barrier function is believed to play a significant role, allowing certain substances to enter the bloodstream and incite immune responses against the body's own tissues. This interplay between gut permeability and autoimmunity underscores the importance of understanding and addressing leaky gut in the context of autoimmune diseases.

a. Celiac Disease and Leaky Gut: Celiac disease, an autoimmune condition triggered by gluten consumption in genetically predisposed individuals, exhibits a profound connection with leaky gut. In celiac patients, gluten damages the intestinal lining, compromising the gut barrier. This breach allows undigested gluten peptides and other substances to leak into the bloodstream, provoking an immune response. The interplay between leaky gut and celiac disease underscores how the impaired gut barrier function contributes to the body's autoimmune response against its own tissues, emphasizing the crucial role of addressing leaky gut in managing this condition effectively.

b. Crohn's Disease and Leaky Gut: Crohn's disease, a type of inflammatory bowel disease, showcases intricate associations with leaky gut. In Crohn's patients, chronic inflammation weakens the intestinal barrier, leading to increased permeability. Harmful bacteria and antigens breach the compromised gut lining, triggering immune responses and exacerbating the inflammation. The synergy between leaky gut and Crohn's disease highlights the significance of understanding and targeting gut barrier integrity in the management of this challenging autoimmune disorder. Addressing the leaky gut component can potentially aid in alleviating the symptoms and prevention of disease progression.

c. Rheumatoid Arthritis and Leaky Gut: Rheumatoid arthritis, a chronic autoimmune disorder primarily affecting joints, has been linked to leaky gut. In individuals with rheumatoid arthritis, a compromised gut barrier allows bacteria and toxins to enter the bloodstream, inciting an inflammatory response. This systemic inflammation aggravates joint inflammation, worsening arthritis symptoms. The intricate relationship between leaky gut and rheumatoid arthritis emphasizes the importance of considering gut health as a contributing factor to the disease process. Addressing leaky gut may offer novel avenues for managing inflammation and improving the overall well-being of individuals living with rheumatoid arthritis.

Recognizing the connection between leaky gut and autoimmune diseases opens avenues for potential therapeutic interventions. Strategies aimed at restoring gut barrier integrity, such as specialized diets, probiotics, and targeted medications, are being explored. Additionally, research is underway to unravel the intricate molecular mechanisms behind leaky gut and its influence on autoimmune responses, paving the way for more targeted and effective treatments.

VINDHYA SINGH

2
CHAPTER
Gut Health

Introduction To Gut Problems

In the intricate tapestry of the human body, the gut plays a vital role, often underestimated and overlooked. Yet, within this unassuming region lies a universe of complexity that affects our overall well-being in ways we are only beginning to comprehend. This book is a gateway into the enigmatic world of gut problems, designed specifically for general readers seeking clarity in the realm of digestive health.

Our digestive system, often referred to as the body's second brain, is a powerhouse of activity. It processes the food we consume, extracting essential nutrients and energy vital for our survival. However, this seemingly straightforward process can sometimes go awry, leading to a myriad of gut-related issues that impact our daily lives. From the discomfort of bloating to the challenges posed by conditions like IBD, celiac disease, and irritable bowel syndrome, understanding these problems is essential for our overall health and happiness.

In the pages that follow, we will embark on a journey to unravel the mysteries of the gut. We will explore the science behind digestion, demystify common digestive diseases, and delve into the intricacies of food sensitivities and their impact. Together, we will navigate the fascinating world of gut healing spices, herbs, and dietary changes that can transform our digestive health.

Furthermore, we will investigate the profound connection between gut health and weight management, uncovering the secrets of appetite regulation, metabolism, and the gut-brain axis. Additionally, we will explore how a healthy gut contributes significantly to our immune system, shielding us from allergies and ensuring optimal nutrient absorption.

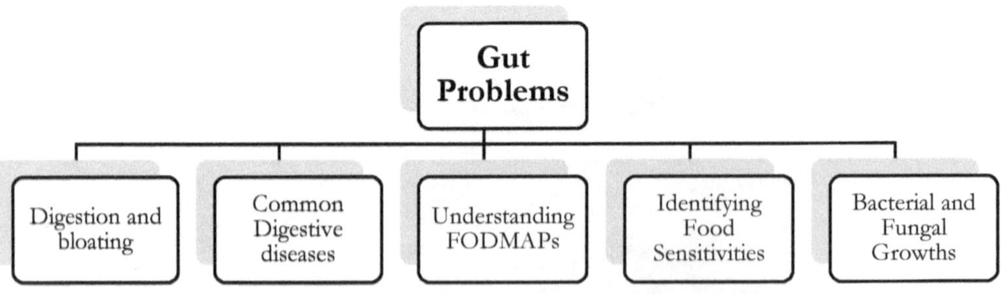

Digestion and bloating

Digestion is the process by which the body breaks down food into smaller components so that nutrients can be absorbed into the bloodstream and used for energy, growth, and repair. Bloating is a feeling of fullness or tightness in the abdomen, often accompanied by visible swelling. It can result from excess gas in the digestive system or other factors, leading to discomfort and a sensation of being overly full. Symptoms of food intolerance, such as impaired digestion, bloating, and stomach pain, could be linked to issues within the gut's bacterial balance.

Certainly! Digestion and bloating are closely related to the gut microbiota, which refers to the diverse community of microorganisms, including bacteria, in the digestive tract. These microorganisms play a crucial role in the process of digestion and can influence the occurrence of bloating. Here's an elaboration on how digestion and bloating are connected to gut microbiota:

i. Digestion and Gut Microbiota:

- **Breakdown of Complex Substances**: The gut microbiota helps break down complex carbohydrates, fibers, and other substances that human digestive enzymes cannot process on their own. Certain bacteria in the gut produce enzymes that assist in breaking down these substances into simpler compounds.

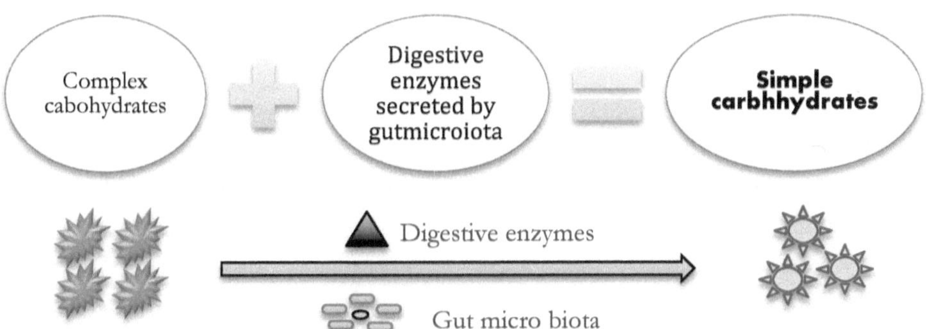

- **Fermentation:** Some components of food, such as dietary fiber, reach the colon undigested. Gut bacteria ferment these substances, producing short-chain fatty acids (SCFAs) and gases like hydrogen and methane. SCFAs serve as an energy source for the cells lining the colon and have various health benefits.

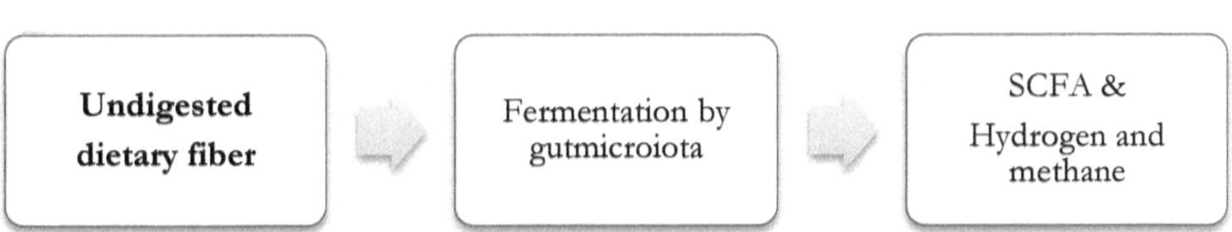

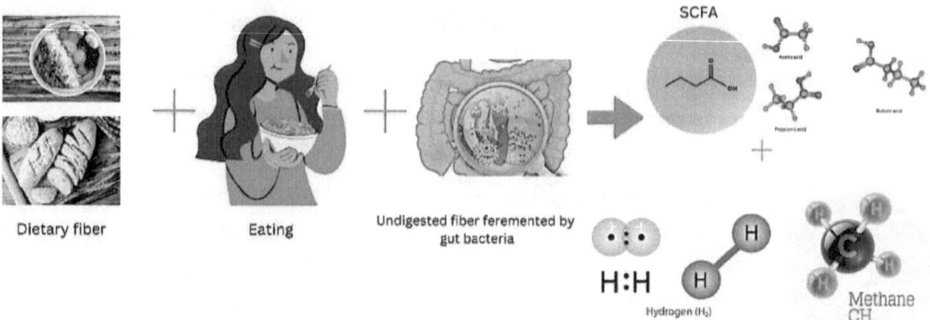

- **Nutrient Absorption**: The gut micro biota aids in the absorption of essential nutrients, such as certain vitamins and minerals, by breaking down food particles and promoting their absorption through the intestinal lining.
- **Protection against Pathogens:** Beneficial bacteria in the gut compete with harmful pathogens for resources and space. They help maintain a balanced and healthy gut environment, reducing the risk of infections and diseases.

ii. Bloating and Gut Micro biota

- **Gas Production:** As mentioned earlier, the fermentation process in the colon produces gases. While some of these gases are absorbed into the bloodstream and expelled through the lungs, excess gas can lead to bloating.
- **Imbalance in Gut Microbiota:** Disruptions in the balance of gut microbiota, known as dysbiosis, can lead to the overgrowth of certain harmful bacteria. This imbalance can result from factors like an unhealthy diet, antibiotics, or stress. Dysbiosis may contribute to excessive gas production and bloating.

- **Food Intolerances:** Certain individuals have food intolerances, such as lactose intolerance or fructose malabsorption, where the gut microbiota struggles to digest specific carbohydrates, leading to bloating and discomfort.
- **Irritable Bowel Syndrome (IBS):** IBS is a functional gastrointestinal disorder characterized by symptoms like bloating, abdominal pain, and altered bowel habits. Changes in the composition and activity of gut microbiota have been observed in individuals with IBS, and these alterations may contribute to bloating.

In summary, a balanced and diverse gut microbiota is essential for proper digestion, nutrient absorption, and protection against gastrointestinal issues. Imbalances in the gut microbiota can lead to problems like bloating.

Common Digestive Diseases:

Digestive diseases are a group of conditions that affect the gastrointestinal tract, which is the system that helps your body digest food and eliminate waste. There are many different types of bowel diseases, Certainly! Let's break down these common digestive diseases in simple terms:

1. IBD (Inflammatory Bowel Disease):

What is it? Inflammatory Bowel Disease is a group of chronic conditions that cause inflammation in the digestive tract.

Symptoms: Abdominal pain, diarrhea, weight loss, and fatigue are common symptoms.

Causes: The exact cause is unknown, but it involves a combination of genetic, environmental, and immune system factors.

Treatment: Treatment aims to reduce inflammation and manage symptoms. Medications and sometimes surgery are used.

Common Types: The two main types are Crohn's disease and ulcerative colitis.

- **Crohn's disease** is an inflammatory bowel disease (IBD) that can affect any part of the gastrointestinal tract, from the mouth to the anus. Symptoms of Crohn's disease can vary depending on the location of the inflammation, but they may include abdominal pain, diarrhea, weight loss, and fever.

- **Ulcerative colitis** is another type of IBD that affects the innermost lining of the colon and rectum. Symptoms of ulcerative colitis may include abdominal pain, bloody diarrhea, weight loss, and fever.

There is no cure for any of these bowel diseases, but there are treatments that can help manage symptoms and improve quality of life. Treatment options may include medication, dietary changes, and lifestyle modifications.

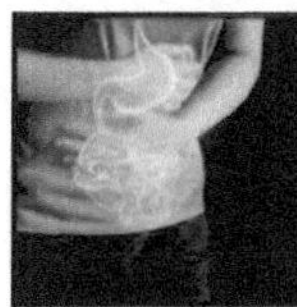

IBD
- Inflammation in the digestive tract.

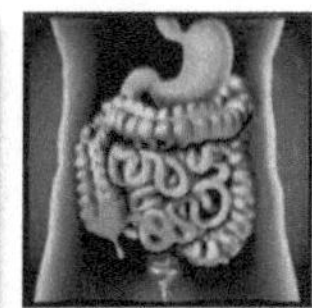

Crohn's disease
- Any part of the digestive tract from mouth to anus, often in patches

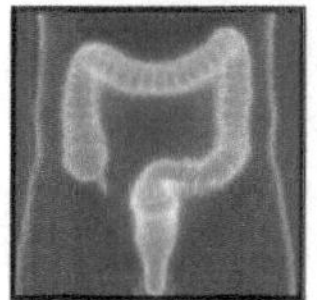

Ulcerative colitis
- Primarily the large intestine and rectum in continuous stretches

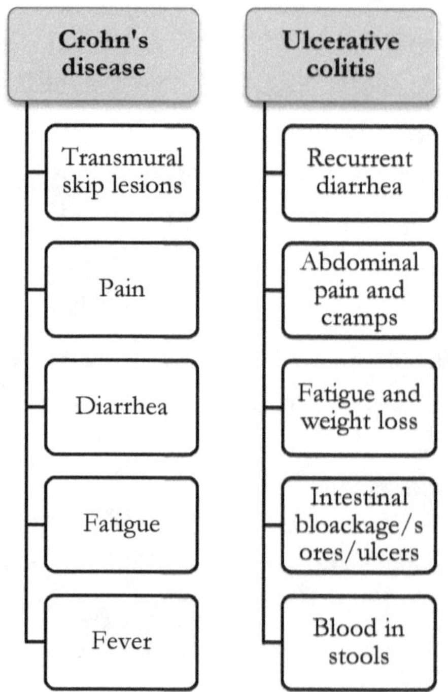

Figure 2 – Inflammation in crohn's disease and ulcerative colitis

Crohn's disease	Ulcerative colitis
Transmural skip lesions	Recurrent diarrhea
Pain	Abdominal pain and cramps
Diarrhea	Fatigue and weight loss
Fatigue	Intestinal bloackage/s ores/ulcers
Fever	Blood in stools

Figure 3 – Symptoms of crohn's disease and ulcerative colitis

2. Celiac Disease:

What is it? Celiac disease is an autoimmune disorder where the ingestion of gluten (a protein found in wheat, barley, and rye) damages the small intestine.

Symptoms: Digestive issues like diarrhea, abdominal pain, and bloating, as well as fatigue and skin rashes are common symptoms.

Causes: Genetic and environmental factors play a role. It's triggered by the consumption of gluten-containing foods.

Treatment: A strict gluten-free diet is the primary treatment. Avoiding gluten-containing foods helps manage symptoms and promotes healing of the intestine.

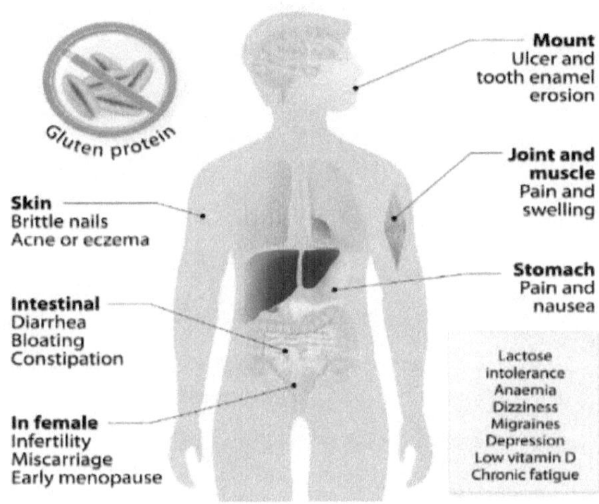

Figure 4 – Symptoms of celiac disease

3. Gastroenteritis:

What is it? Gastroenteritis is inflammation of the stomach and intestines, usually caused by viral or bacterial infections.

Symptoms: Nausea, vomiting, diarrhea, abdominal cramps, and fever are common symptoms.

Causes: Viruses (like norovirus) and bacteria (like Salmonella) from contaminated food or water are common causes.

Treatment: Rest, staying hydrated, and sometimes medication to manage symptoms. In severe cases, medical attention may be needed.

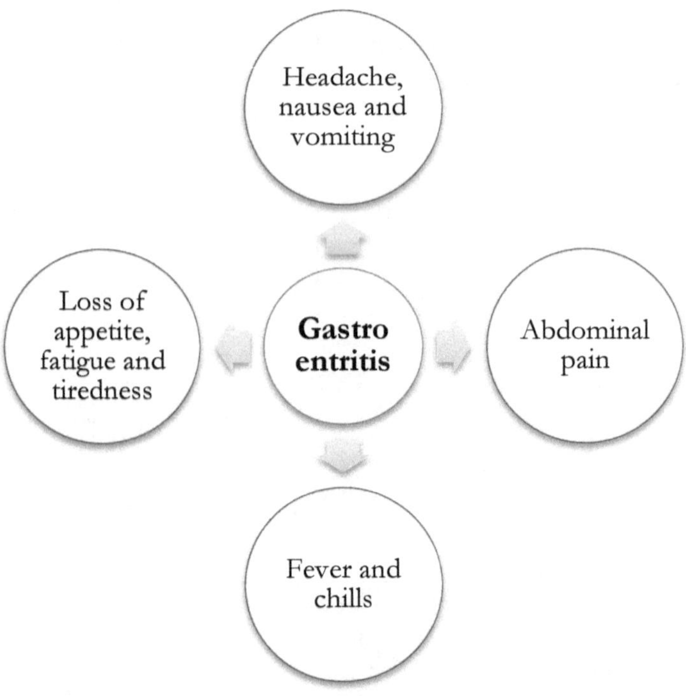

Figure 5 – Symptoms of gastroenteritis

4. IBS (Irritable Bowel Syndrome)

What is it? Irritable Bowel Syndrome is a functional gastrointestinal disorder characterized by abdominal pain and changes in bowel habits without any visible signs of damage or inflammation in the digestive tract.

Symptoms: Abdominal pain, bloating, and changes in bowel habits (diarrhea, constipation, or both) are common symptoms.

Causes: The exact cause is unknown, but factors like sensitive intestines, abnormal muscle contractions, and gut-brain interaction are thought to contribute.

Treatment: Dietary changes, stress management, and medications are used to alleviate symptoms. It's a chronic condition managed over time.

It's important to consult a healthcare professional if you suspect you have any of these conditions, as they can provide proper diagnosis and guidance for managing the symptoms.

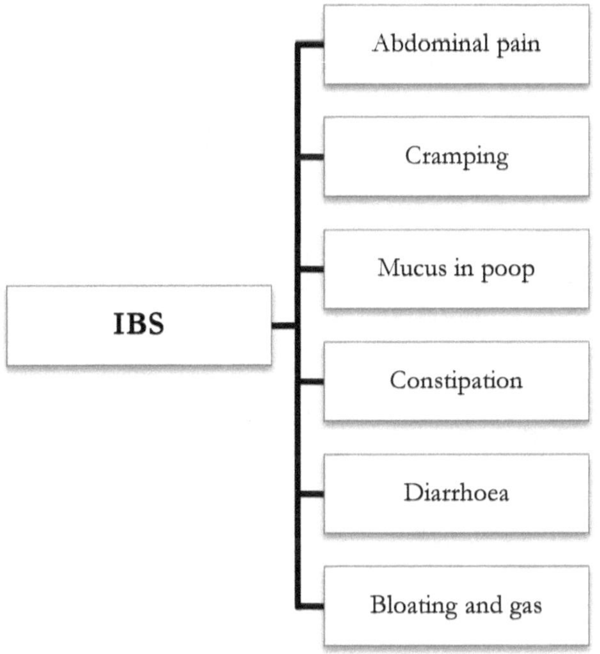

Figure 6 – Symptoms of IBS

3. Understanding FODMAPs

FODMAPs (Fermentable Oligosaccharides, Disaccharides, Monosaccharides, and Polyols) are types of carbohydrates that can cause digestive discomfort in some people. Here's a simple explanation:

What are FODMAPs? FODMAPs are specific types of sugars and fibers found in various foods. Some individuals have difficulty digesting these carbohydrates, which can lead to symptoms like bloating, gas, and stomach pain.

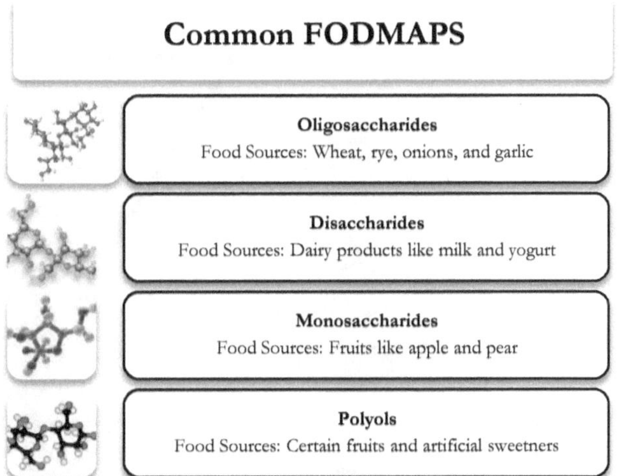

Common FODMAPs

How FODMAPs Affect Digestion?

For some people, FODMAPs can ferment in the gut, causing gas and bloating. People with irritable bowel syndrome (IBS) or other digestive disorders might benefit from a low-FODMAP diet to reduce these symptoms.

4. Identifying food sensitivities

Identifying food sensitivities involves understanding how certain foods can trigger adverse reactions in some individuals. Here's a simple explanation:

What are Food Sensitivities?

Food sensitivities occur when the body has a negative response to certain foods. Unlike allergies, which involve the immune system, sensitivities are often related to the digestive system and can cause symptoms such as bloating, headaches, or fatigue after eating specific foods.

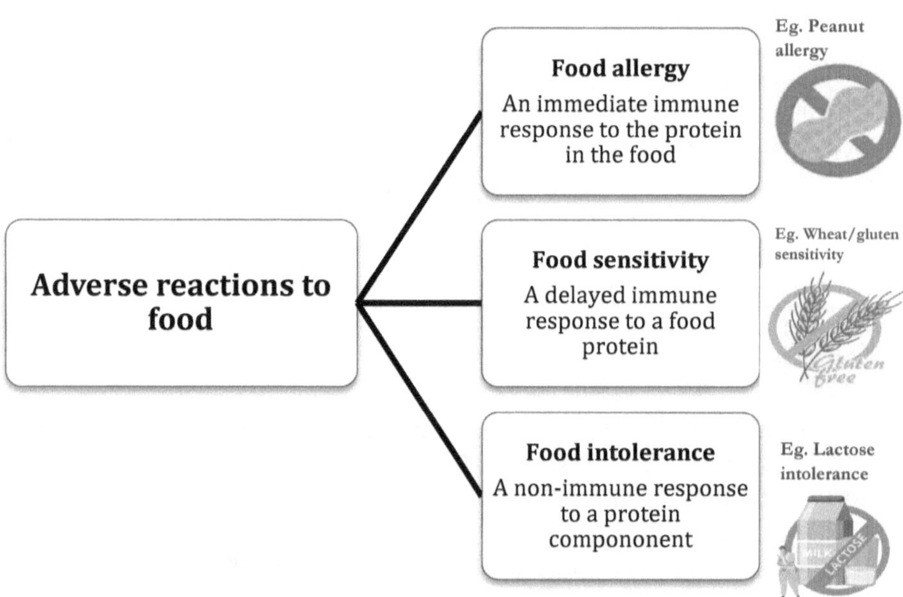

Common Methods for Identifying Food Sensitivities:

a. Elimination Diet: This method involves removing suspected trigger foods from your diet for a certain period (usually a few weeks) and then reintroducing them one at a time to observe any adverse reactions.

b. Food Sensitivity Tests: Various tests, such as IgG (Immunoglobulin G) blood tests or hair analysis, claim to identify food sensitivities. However, their accuracy and reliability are often debated in the scientific community. It's important to note that consulting a healthcare professional or a registered dietitian is crucial when trying to identify food sensitivities. They can provide personalized guidance and ensure you follow safe and evidence-based methods to manage your diet effectively.

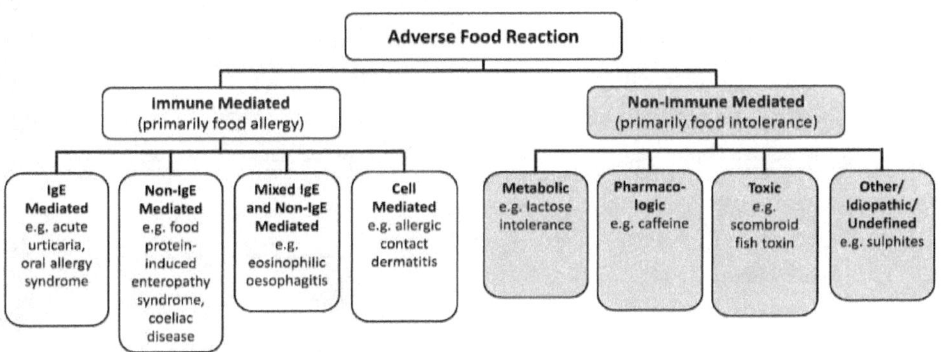

Figure 7 – Identifying food sensitivities

5. Bacterial and fungal growth

Let's delve a bit deeper into bacterial and fungal growth in the gut and their implications for our health:

Bacterial Growths in the Gut: The Gut micro biota plays a crucial role in digestion, nutrient absorption, and even influencing our immune system. In a healthy gut, there's a balance between beneficial bacteria and potentially harmful ones. However, factors like a poor diet, stress, illness, or antibiotic use can disrupt this balance. When harmful bacteria overgrow, they can cause problems such as bacterial infections, leading to symptoms like diarrhea, abdominal pain, and inflammation. Certain conditions like Small Intestinal Bacterial Overgrowth (SIBO) involve the excessive growth of bacteria in the small intestine, interfering with normal digestion.

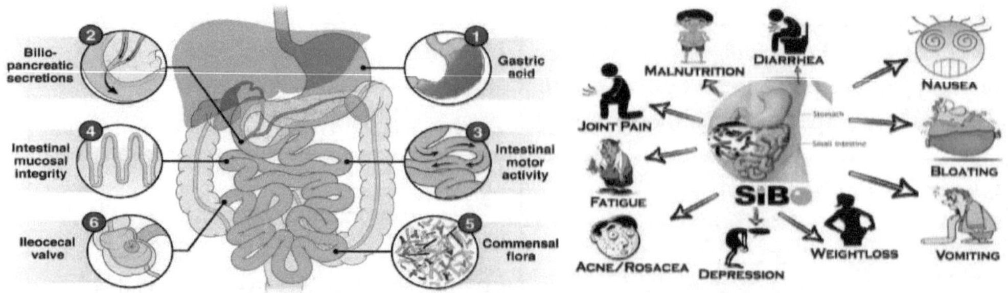

Figure 8 – Pathophysiology and symptoms of SIBO

Fungal Growths in the Gut: Fungi, particularly Candida species, are also present in the gut. Candida is a type of yeast that is normally kept in check by the immune system and other beneficial bacteria in the gut. However, under certain conditions, such as a weakened immune system, prolonged antibiotic use, or a high-sugar diet, Candida can overgrow, leads to a condition known as *Candidiasis* or yeast overgrowth. Candidiasis can cause various health issues, including oral thrush, digestive problems, and even systemic infections in severe cases. Symptoms might include persistent fatigue, bloating, and recurrent fungal infections.

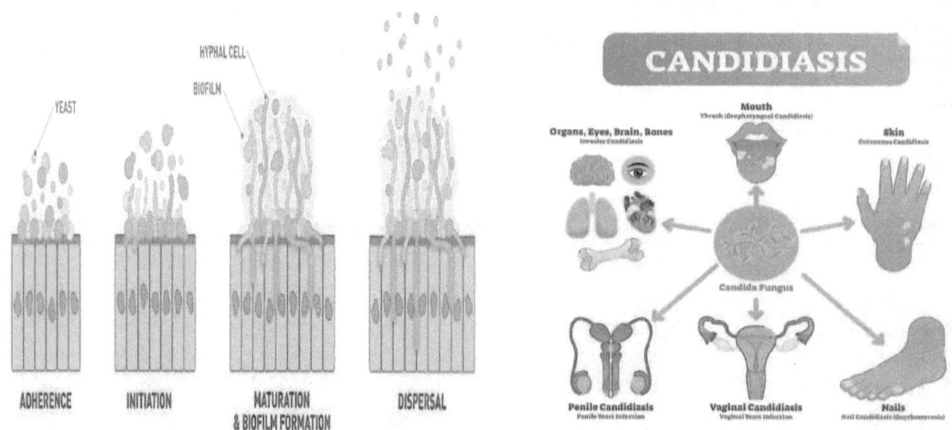

Figure 9 – Pathophysiology and symptoms of candidiasis

Implications for Health:

Both bacterial and fungal imbalances in the gut can impact our overall health and well-being. Maintaining a healthy gut balance through a balanced diet rich in fiber, prebiotics, and probiotics, as well as managing stress, can support the proper functioning of the gut microbiota and help prevent imbalances. Understanding these complex interactions between our body and the microorganisms within us is crucial for developing effective strategies for managing gut-related health problems and promoting overall health.

VINDHYA SINGH

II. Healing The Gut Naturally

a. Gut Healing Spices and Herbs (Nuskhe):

In the journey towards holistic well-being, the significance of maintaining a healthy gut cannot be overstated. Our digestive system plays a crucial role in ensuring that the nutrients from the food we consume are absorbed effectively, contributing to overall health. In this exploration of gut healing, we'll delve into the world of traditional remedies, focusing on spices and herbs, or "Nuskhe" as they are known in various cultures. These natural wonders have been celebrated for their ability to promote gut health, and among them are Aloe Vera, Licorice (Mulethi), and Hing.

1. Aloe Vera: The Soothing Succulent

Aloe Vera, often recognized for its external applications in skincare, is equally potent when it comes to internal healing. This succulent plant has a long history of use in traditional medicine, revered for its ability to promote gut health. The gel found within the Aloe Vera leaves contains a rich array of vitamins, minerals, and antioxidants that can aid in soothing and repairing the digestive tract. Aloe vera has natural anti-inflammatory and healing properties that can soothe the digestive tract. Aloe vera is a succulent plant known for its medicinal properties. It can help in reducing irritation and promoting the healing of the gut lining

Aloe Vera's anti-inflammatory properties are particularly beneficial for individuals dealing with digestive issues such as irritable bowel syndrome (IBS) or inflammatory bowel diseases (IBD). Its soothing effects can alleviate discomfort and promote a healthier gut environment. Incorporating Aloe Vera into your routine can be as simple as adding its gel to smoothies or opting for Aloe Vera juice, which is readily available in health food stores.

2. Licorice (Mulethi): Sweet Relief for the Gut

Licorice root has been traditionally used for its anti-inflammatory and soothing effects on the gut lining. Licorice root, or Mulethi in Hindi, It contains glycyrrhizin, which has anti-inflammatory effects. Licorice can help in reducing inflammation in the stomach and intestines, providing relief from digestive discomfort. Licorice used in many traditional medicinal practices and it is not just a flavorful treat but also a powerful herb with digestive benefits. The root of the licorice plant contains compounds that possess anti-inflammatory and anti-ulcer properties, making it a go-to remedy for various gastrointestinal issues.

Mulethi is known to stimulate the production of mucin, a substance that forms a protective layer in the stomach and intestines. This protective barrier helps shield the delicate tissues from the harmful effects of stomach acid, promoting a healthier gut lining. Additionally, licorice has been studied for its potential in managing symptoms of acid reflux and heartburn.

Incorporating licorice into your routine can be done through licorice tea or by chewing on licorice root sticks. However, it's essential to use licorice in moderation, as excessive consumption may lead to adverse effects.

3. Hing: The Aromatic Gut Ally

Hing, also known as asafoetida, is a pungent spice derived from the resin of the Ferula plant. While it is renowned for adding a distinctive flavor to culinary dishes, its medicinal properties make it a valuable asset for gut health. In traditional medicine, hing has been used to address digestive issues, including bloating, gas, and indigestion. Hing, has anti-flatulent and digestive properties, helping in reducing bloating and gas. Hing is a pungent spice used in Indian cuisine. It can help in relieving bloating, gas, and indigestion by reducing excessive gas formation in the digestive system.

Hing contains compounds that exhibit anti-flatulent and anti-spasmodic properties,

making it effective in reducing gas and bloating. Additionally, its ability to enhance digestive enzyme activity aids in the smoother breakdown of food in the stomach, promoting overall digestive wellness. To incorporate hing into your diet, it can be used in various recipes, especially those featuring lentils, beans, and vegetables. Adding a pinch of hing to your cooking not only enhances the flavor but also contributes to a healthier digestive experience.

In the pursuit of gut health, embracing the healing properties of nature through spices and herbs can be a transformative journey. Aloe Vera, Licorice (Mulethi), and Hing stand out as formidable allies in this quest, offering a blend of traditional wisdom and scientific validation. Whether sipped in a cup of tea, added to a recipe, or integrated into daily rituals, these gut-healing nuskhe have the potential to make a significant impact on digestive well-being. As we continue to explore the synergies between traditional remedies and modern science, the power of nature's pharmacy becomes increasingly evident, reminding us that sometimes, the path to wellness is rooted in the simplicity of the earth's offerings.

b. Dietary Changes for Gut Health:

The saying, "You are what you eat," holds a profound truth, especially when it comes to the health of your gut. The gut, often referred to as the second brain, plays a crucial role in maintaining overall well-being. In this exploration of dietary changes for gut health, we'll uncover the importance of incorporating fiber, prebiotics, and probiotics into your diet, understanding the role of digestive enzymes, and embracing strategies for repairing the intestinal barrier.

1. Importance of Fiber, Prebiotics, and Probiotics: Building a Strong Foundation

Fiber, prebiotics, and probiotics promote a healthy gut by supporting beneficial bacteria and regular bowel movements. These components support a healthy gut environment, aiding in digestion and boosting the immune system.

Fiber: Think of fiber as the broom for your digestive system. Found in fruits, vegetables, and whole grains, fiber adds bulk to your stool and helps it move through the intestines, preventing constipation. It also serves as food for beneficial gut bacteria, promoting a balanced and diverse microbiome.

Prebiotics: Prebiotics are like the fertilizer for the good bacteria in your gut. Prebiotics are non-digestible fibers that nourish beneficial gut bacteria. They are non-digestible fibers that nourish and support the growth of probiotics. Foods rich in prebiotics include garlic, onions, bananas, and asparagus. Including these in your diet helps maintain a thriving community of beneficial bacteria in your gut.

Probiotics: Probiotics are the friendly bacteria that confer numerous health benefits. Probiotics are live beneficial bacteria found in fermented foods like yogurt like yogurt, kefir, sauerkraut, and kimchi. Probiotics aid digestion, strengthen the immune system, and contribute to a balanced gut flora. Including these probiotic-rich foods regularly can positively impact your gut health.

2. Digestive Enzymes: Unlocking Nutrient Absorption

Digestive enzymes are like the key to unlocking the nutrients in your food. Produced by the body and found in certain foods, these enzymes break down complex nutrients into simpler forms, making them easier for the body to absorb. Digestive enzymes aid the breakdown of food, improving digestion and nutrient absorption. Digestive enzymes help break down carbohydrates, proteins, and fats in the digestive system, making nutrients easier to absorb. They can aid individuals who have difficulty digesting certain foods, promoting better digestion and reducing discomfort

Natural Sources: Pineapple and papaya contain enzymes like bromelain and papain, respectively, which aid in protein digestion. Including these fruits in your diet can complement your body's natural enzyme production.

Supplements: In some cases, especially if you experience digestive issues, digestive enzyme supplements can be beneficial. These supplements provide additional support in breaking down carbohydrates, proteins, and fats, promoting optimal nutrient absorption and reducing discomfort after meals.

3. Intestinal Barrier Repair: Strengthening the Gut Wall

The gut has a protective barrier that controls what gets absorbed into the bloodstream. When this barrier is compromised, it can lead to inflammation and various digestive issues. Certain dietary strategies can help repair and maintain the integrity of the intestinal barrier.. The intestinal barrier, often likened to a fortress, acts as the first line of defense against harmful substances and pathogens trying to enter our bloodstream. Maintaining the integrity of this barrier is crucial for optimal digestive health. Let's explore the roles of Collagen, Glutamine, Glycine, and Zinc in supporting the repair and fortification of the intestinal barrier. These substances support the intestinal barrier, preventing harmful substances from entering the bloodstream. Collagen, glutamine, glycine, and zinc are essential nutrients that support the intestinal barrier. Glutamine is an amino acid that promotes gut cell regeneration. Glycine helps in the synthesis of collagen, and zinc supports the healing of the intestinal lining

1. Collagen: The Foundation of Gut Integrity

Collagen is a protein that serves as the building block for various connective tissues in our body, including the gut lining. It provides structural support and helps maintain the integrity of the mucosal layer, which is vital for a healthy digestive system.

How does Collagen support intestinal barrier repair? The gut's mucosal layer acts as a protective barrier, preventing harmful substances from crossing into the bloodstream. Collagen plays a significant role in maintaining and repairing this mucosal layer. It helps in the formation of tight junctions, which are like gatekeepers that regulate the passage of molecules.

Adequate collagen levels contribute to a robust gut lining, reducing the risk of inflammation and leaky gut.

Sources of Collagen: You can naturally boost your collagen levels by including bone broth, chicken skin, fish, and collagen-rich foods in your diet. Additionally, collagen supplements are available for those looking for an extra boost to support gut health. **Bone Broth** is rich in collagen and amino acids, bone broth supports the repair of the gut lining. It helps maintain the mucosal layer, reducing inflammation and promoting a healthy gut environment.

2. Glutamine: The Healing Amino Acid:

Glutamine is an amino acid, a fundamental building block of proteins, and it plays a crucial role in various bodily functions, including intestinal barrier repair.

How does Glutamine support intestinal barrier repair? The cells lining the intestine rely heavily on glutamine for energy. When the gut is damaged or under stress during inflammation, the demand for glutamine increases. Glutamine helps in the regeneration and repair of the intestinal lining, promoting the growth of healthy tissues and aiding in the closure of any gaps or wounds in the mucosa. This reparative process contributes to a stronger and more resilient gut barrier.

Sources of Glutamine: Foods rich in glutamine include cabbage, spinach, parsley, and other green leafy vegetables. Additionally, incorporating protein-rich foods like poultry, fish, and dairy into your diet can contribute to your glutamine intake. Glutamine is an amino acid crucial for the repair of the intestinal lining and can be beneficial for maintaining a robust gut barrier.

3. Glycine: The Gut Soother

Glycine is another amino acid, known for its role in supporting various physiological functions in the body, including the health of the digestive system.

How does Glycine support intestinal barrier repair? Glycine has anti-inflammatory properties and acts as a precursor to collagen synthesis. This means that it not only helps in reducing inflammation in the gut but also contributes to the formation of collagen, reinforcing the structural integrity of the mucosal layer. By soothing inflammation and aiding in tissue repair, glycine plays a vital role in supporting a healthy gut barrier.

Sources of Glycine: Dietary sources of glycine include meat, fish, dairy products, and legumes. Bone broth, which contains collagen and glycine, can be a particularly beneficial addition to your diet for gut health.

4. Zinc: The Guardian of Gut Defense

Zinc is a trace mineral that plays a crucial role in various physiological processes, including immune function and wound healing.

How does Zinc support intestinal barrier repair? Zinc is involved in the maintenance and repair of the intestinal lining. It promotes the production of proteins that contribute to the structure of the gut barrier, including those involved in the formation of tight junctions. Zinc's ability to modulate immune responses also contributes to a balanced and well-functioning gut defense system.

Sources of Zinc: Zinc is found in various foods, including meat, nuts, seeds, and dairy products. Including a diverse range of zinc-rich foods in your diet helps ensure an adequate supply of this essential mineral for gut health.

Omega-3 Fatty Acids: Found in fatty fish like salmon, flaxseeds, and walnuts, omega-3 fatty acids have anti-inflammatory properties that contribute to a healthier gut lining. Including these foods in your diet helps support the overall integrity of the digestive tract.

In nurturing the health of your gut, understanding the roles of Collagen, Glutamine, Glycine, and Zinc in intestinal barrier repair empowers you to make informed dietary choices. These elements work synergistically to strengthen and fortify the gut lining, reducing the risk of inflammation and promoting a resilient defense against potential threats. Incorporating a variety of nutrient-rich foods that support these components can be a simple yet effective strategy for promoting a healthier gut and overall well-being. Embarking on a journey towards better gut health doesn't have to be complicated. Simple dietary changes can pave the way for a happier tummy and overall well-being. By recognizing the significance of fiber, prebiotics, and probiotics in building a strong foundation, understanding the role of digestive enzymes in nutrient absorption, and embracing strategies for intestinal barrier repair, you empower yourself to make choices that positively impact your digestive health.

Remember, it's not about making drastic changes overnight but incorporating these elements gradually into your daily meals. Your gut, often overlooked but incredibly influential, will thank you for the nourishment and care you provide. As you navigate the realm of dietary choices for gut health, consider it a journey of self-discovery, where you learn to listen to your body and cultivate habits that support a thriving digestive system. After all, a happy gut lays the groundwork for a healthier and happier you.

c. High Fiber Benefits- Isabgol:

Isabgol (psyllium husk) is rich in soluble fiber, aiding in softening stools and promoting regular bowel movements. Isabgol, or psyllium husk, is a natural source of soluble fiber. It absorbs water and forms a gel-like substance in the intestines. This softens stools, making them easier to pass. Isabgol helps in relieving constipation and promoting regular bowel movements.

d. Understanding Short Chain Fatty Acids (Butyrate):

In the intricate world of gut health, there's a group of tiny heroes known as Short Chain Fatty Acids (SCFAs), with Butyrate leading the charge. These microscopic compounds play a crucial role in maintaining the balance and well-being of your digestive system. Short-chain fatty acids, particularly butyrate, are produced by gut bacteria during the fermentation of dietary fiber and play a vital role in gut health. Butyrate, a prominent SCFA, serves as the primary energy source for the cells lining the colon. It also has anti-inflammatory properties, supporting a healthy gut lining and overall guts health

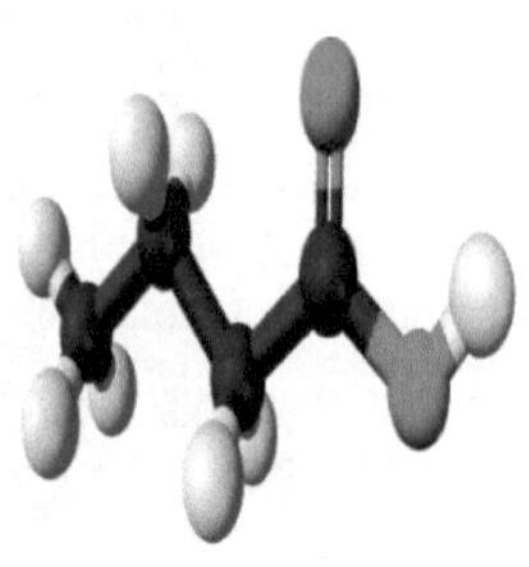

What are Short Chain Fatty Acids (SCFAs)?

SCFAs are small, water-soluble molecules produced when dietary fiber is fermented by the beneficial bacteria in your gut. They are like the beneficial by-products of the teamwork between your diet and the friendly bacteria in your digestive system. Among these SCFAs, Butyrate stands out as a key player in promoting gut health.

The Role of Butyrate in Gut Health:

1. Energy Source for Colon Cells: Butyrate is not just a bystander; it plays a hands-on role in nourishing the cells lining your colon. These cells, also known as colonocytes, use Butyrate as their primary energy source. By providing this energy, Butyrate supports the integrity and function of the colon lining, contributing to a healthy and well-maintained digestive tract.	**2. Anti-Inflammatory Effects:** Inflammation in the gut can lead to a variety of digestive issues. Butyrate, however, steps in as an anti-inflammatory agent. It helps to calm down inflammation, reducing the risk of conditions such as inflammatory bowel diseases (IBD) and promoting an environment where your gut can thrive.
3. Maintaining a Balanced Microbiome: Human gut is a bustling ecosystem of bacteria, and the balance of this microbiome is essential for optimal health. Butyrate plays a role in maintaining this delicate balance by supporting the growth of beneficial bacteria while inhibiting the overgrowth of harmful microbes. This balance contributes to a resilient and diverse microbiome.	**4. Regulating the Immune System:** Butyrate doesn't stop at supporting the gut; it extends its influence to the immune system. By modulating immune responses, Butyrate helps prevent unnecessary immune reactions and ensures that the immune system functions in a balanced and controlled manner. This regulatory role contributes to overall gut health by promoting immune harmony.

Sources of Butyrate:

Butyrate is produced in the gut through the fermentation of dietary fiber; there are specific foods that can enhance its levels:

Dietary Fiber: Whole grains, fruits, vegetables, and legumes are rich in dietary fiber. Consuming a diet high in fiber provides the necessary substrate for the production of Butyrate by gut bacteria.

Resistant Starch: Found in certain foods like green bananas, legumes, and some grains, resistant starch serves as another source for Butyrate production in the gut.

Fermented Foods: Including fermented foods in your diet, such as yogurt, kefir, and sauerkraut, can indirectly support Butyrate production by fostering a healthy gut microbiome.

In the complex world of gut health, understanding the role of Short Chain Fatty Acids, particularly Butyrate, sheds light on the fascinating interplay between your diet, gut bacteria, and overall well-being. By recognizing Butyrate as a crucial player in energy provision, inflammation reduction, microbiome balance, and immune regulation, you can make informed choices to support a happy and healthy gut. Incorporating fiber-rich foods, resistant starch, and fermented goodies into your diet not only provides a banquet for your taste buds but also nourishes your gut's tiny heroes. So, the next time you savor a fiber-packed meal or enjoy a spoonful of yogurt, know that you're not just pleasing your palate but also fostering a thriving community of Butyrate and other beneficial compounds in your gut – the unsung guardians of your tummy's well-being.

e. Avoiding processed foods and sugar:

Avoiding processed foods and sugar is essential for maintaining a healthy stomach. Here's why in a simple way:

Processed Foods: Processed foods often contain additives, preservatives, and high levels of unhealthy fats and sodium. These artificial ingredients can irritate your stomach lining and disrupt your digestive system. Eating too many processed foods may lead to stomachaches, bloating, and other digestive issues.

Sugar: Too much sugar, especially added sugars found in sweets, sugary drinks, and processed snacks, can upset the balance of bacteria in your gut. This imbalance can cause discomfort, gas, and diarrhea. Sugary foods and drinks can also contribute to weight gain, which might put pressure on your stomach and lead to acid reflux.

Why Avoiding Them Is Important?

- **Digestive Comfort:** Cutting down on processed foods and sugar reduces the likelihood of stomachaches, bloating, and indigestion. Your stomach will feel more comfortable overall.

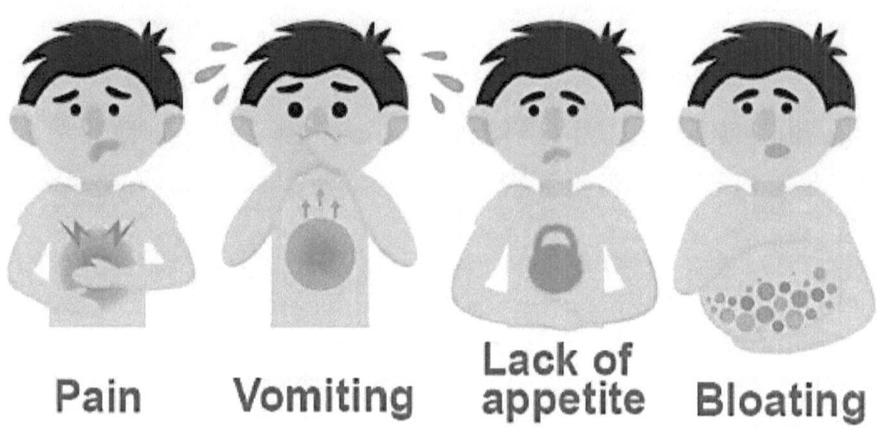

- **Balanced Gut:** Avoiding excessive sugar helps maintain a healthy balance of good and bad bacteria in your gut. This balance is crucial for proper digestion and overall well-being.

A healthy bacteria balance
means that the good bacteria
overpower the bad bacteria

- **Weight Management:** Limiting sugar intake can help with weight management. Maintaining a healthy weight is important for preventing stomach-related issues like acid reflux.

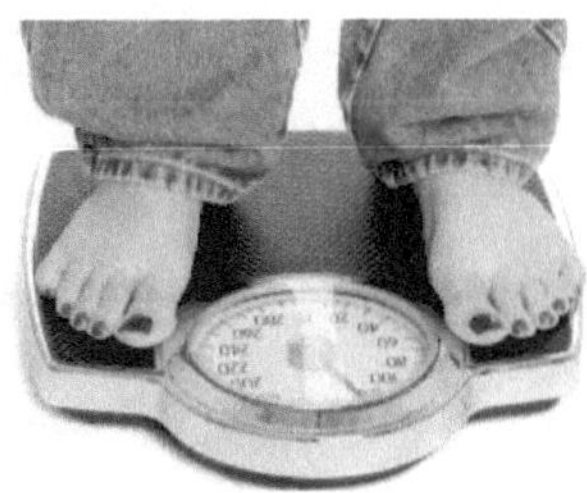

Simple Tips

Read the label first

Cook at home

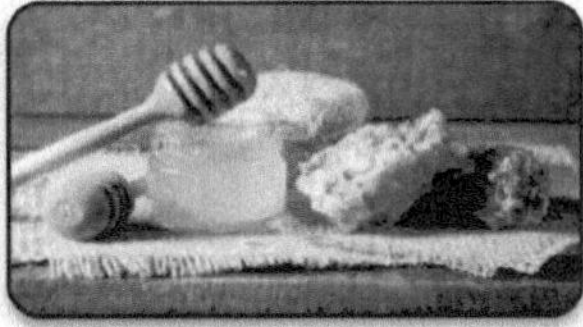

Natural sweetners

- **Read Labels:** Avoid foods with long lists of ingredients you can't pronounce. Opt for whole foods like fruits, vegetables, lean proteins, and whole grains.
- **Cook at Home:** Prepare meals at home using fresh ingredients. Homemade meals are often healthier and allow you to control what goes into your food.
- **Choose Natural Sweeteners:** If you have a sweet tooth, opt for natural sweeteners like honey or maple syrup in moderation. These options are less processed than refined sugars.

By avoiding processed foods and sugar, you're giving your stomach the chance to function at its best, leading to a happier, healthier digestive system. It's important to note that while these natural remedies and dietary changes can be beneficial, individual responses vary. Consulting a healthcare professional or a registered dietitian is recommended for personalized advice tailored to specific health needs and conditions.

III. Gut Health & Weight Loss:

a. Appetite Regulation and Food Cravings: A healthy gut helps regulate your appetite and cravings. Good bacteria in your gut can influence hormones that control hunger, making you feel full and satisfied after meals. When your gut is balanced, you're less likely to overeat or crave unhealthy foods. When the gut is balanced, it sends signals to the brain that regulate hunger and fullness. This balance is maintained by beneficial bacteria in the gut, which help in controlling our food intake and preventing overeating.

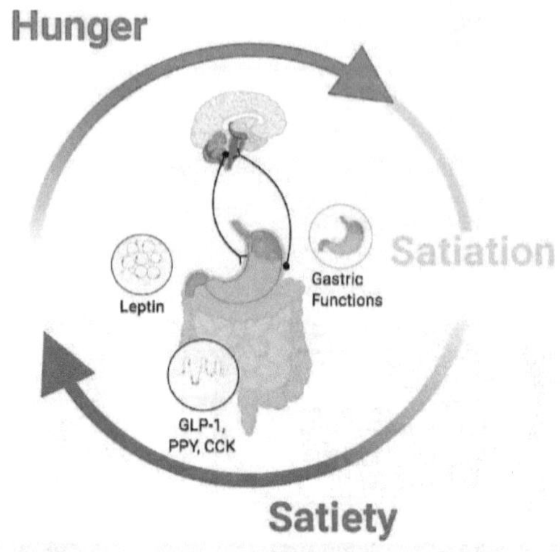

Figure 10 – Homeostatic regulation of food intake

b. Good Probiotic Strains for Fat Loss: Certain probiotics, like *Lactobacillus* and *Bifidobacterium* strains, have been linked to supporting weight loss. These probiotics help maintain a balanced gut environment, which can aid in the process of losing excess body fat.

c. Metabolism and Its Connection to Gut Health: A well-functioning gut supports a healthy metabolism, which is essential for burning calories efficiently. Probiotics can influence metabolism and energy expenditure, potentially helping in weight management. The gut microbiota helps break down food and absorb nutrients, influencing our body's metabolism. When the gut is in good condition, it aids in proper digestion, absorption, and energy utilization, all of which are essential for a healthy metabolism.

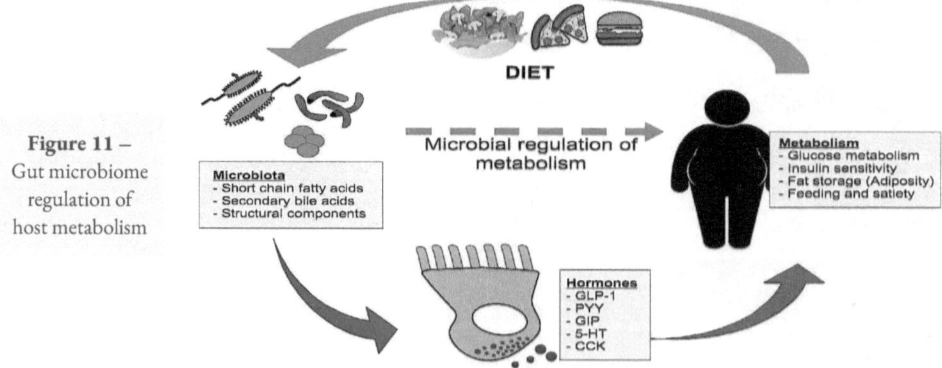

Figure 11 – Gut microbiome regulation of host metabolism

d. Gut-Brain Axis: Impact on Mood and Weight Management:

The gut-brain axis refers to the connection between your gut and brain. A healthy gut positively impacts your mood and stress levels, which can affect weight management. Stress and mood imbalances can lead to unhealthy eating habits and weight gain. Additionally, it influences our food choices and cravings, which can also impact the weight management. A balanced gut can contribute to better emotional health and improved weight control.

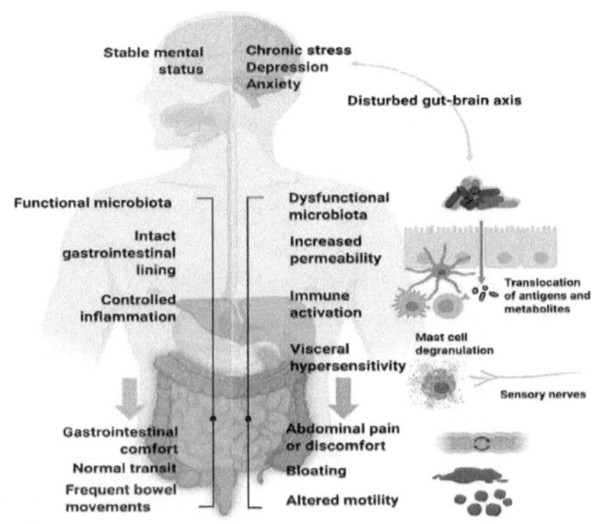

Figure 12 – Stable and disturbed Gut brain axis

e. Importance of Hydration for Gut Health:

Staying hydrated is crucial for gut health. Water helps in the digestion and absorption of nutrients. It also maintains the mucosal lining of the intestines, preventing constipation and promoting overall gut well-being Taking care of your gut through a balanced diet, probiotics, hydration, and mindful eating can contribute significantly to your overall health and weight management efforts.

Figure 13 – Hydration for gut health importance

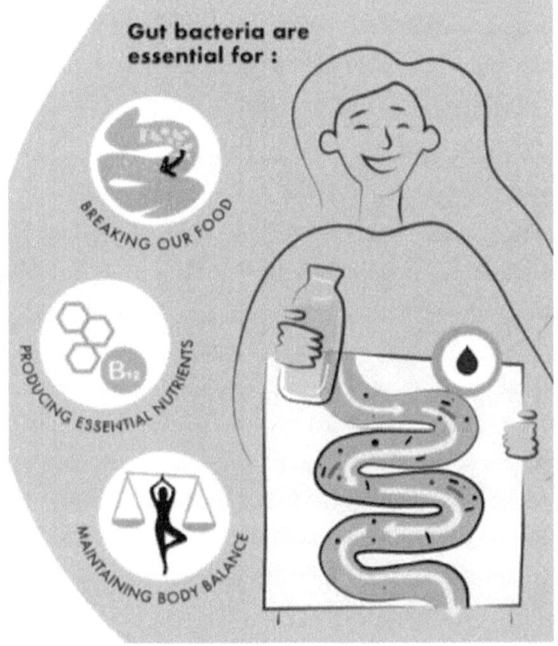

IV. Gut Health And Immune Health

a. Gut and Immune System Interaction: Your gut and immune system are closely connected. The gut houses trillions of bacteria, known as the gut microbiota, which play a vital role in supporting your immune system. These friendly bacteria help your body recognizes harmful invaders and fight off infections. A balanced gut with a variety of beneficial bacteria contributes to a strong and efficient immune response.

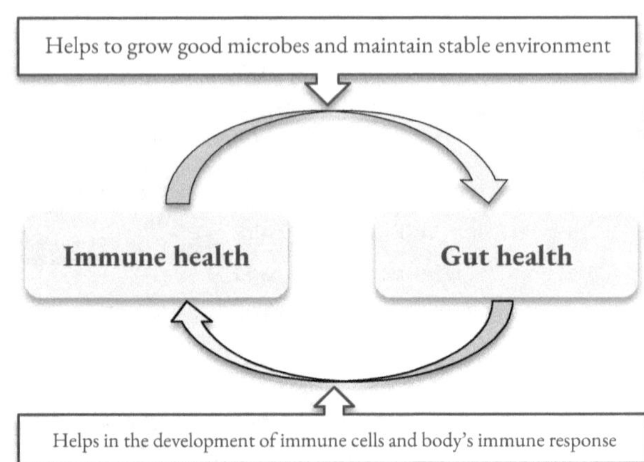

b. Allergies: Connection to Gut Health:

The health of your gut can influence your susceptibility to allergies. A well-balanced gut helps regulate the immune system, reducing the likelihood of developing allergies. When the gut microbiota is imbalanced, it may lead to an overactive immune response, making you more prone to allergic reactions.

c. Addressing Nutrient Absorption Issues: A healthy gut is essential for proper nutrient absorption. The lining of your intestines contains tiny hair-like structures called villi, which absorb nutrients from the food you eat. If your gut is compromised due to inflammation or imbalances in the gut microbiota, it can hinder the absorption of essential nutrients, leading to deficiencies.

Understanding the intricacies of gut health is essential for overall well-being. This comprehensive guide has shed light on the vital role of a healthy gut, offering insights into healing methods and practical maintenance strategies. By embracing a balanced diet, probiotics, and mindful lifestyle choices, individuals can nurture their gut health, leading to improved digestion, enhanced immune function, and better overall health. Empowered with this knowledge, readers can embark on a journey towards a healthier and more vibrant life through optimal gut health. By nurturing a healthy gut through a balanced diet rich in fiber, probiotics, and hydration, you can support your immune system and reduce the risk of allergies.

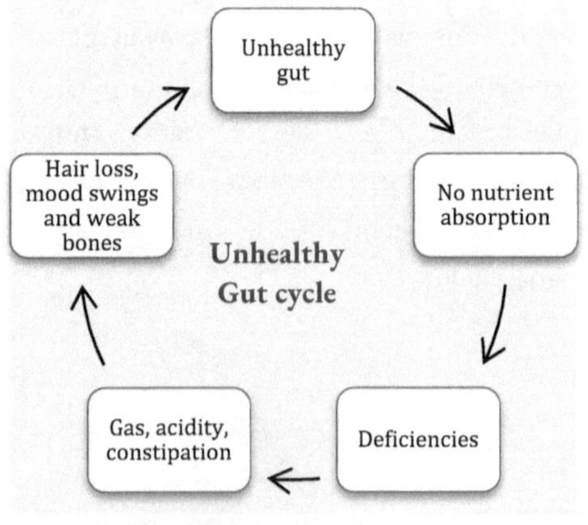

A Journey Into Gut Flora And Repopulation

In the intricate world within our digestive system lies a bustling community of microorganisms known as gut flora or microbiota. This diverse ecosystem, comprised of trillions of bacteria, viruses, fungi, and other microbes, plays a pivotal role in our overall health and well-being. Understanding the importance of a thriving gut flora and how to slowly repopulate it can pave the way for a resilient and balanced internal garden.

The Significance of Gut Flora

Our gut flora is like a bustling city, jam-packed with life and activity. These microscopic inhabitants aren't just passive bystanders; they actively contribute to various physiological functions. They aid in the digestion of food, extract nutrients, synthesize vitamins, and play a crucial role in maintaining a robust immune system. Harmonious balances of these microorganisms are fundamental to gut health, influencing everything from our digestive comfort to our mental well-being.

Factors Impacting Gut Flora:

Modern lifestyles, characterized by processed foods, stress, antibiotics, and environmental factors, can disrupt the delicate equilibrium of our gut flora. Antibiotics, while essential for treating infections, can inadvertently wipe out both harmful and beneficial bacteria, leaving our internal cityscape in disarray. Unhealthy diets, high in sugar and low in fiber, create an environment that favors the growth of less beneficial microbes, further altering the landscape of our gut.

How to Repopulate Gut Flora?

The journey to repopulate and restore balance to our gut flora is not about overnight transformations but rather a gradual and intentional process. Here are some gentle steps to nurture your gut garden:

- **Diversify Your Plate:** Introduce a variety of plant-based foods to your diet. Each type of plant food provides unique fibers that nourish different groups of bacteria. A colorful and diverse plate means a rich and varied gut ecosystem.

- **Embrace Fermented Foods:** Incorporate naturally fermented foods into your meals. Yogurt, kefir, sauerkraut, kimchi, and miso are examples of probiotic-rich foods that introduce live beneficial bacteria to your gut. These friendly microbes can help restore balance.

- **Mindful Antibiotic Use:** When prescribed antibiotics, follow your healthcare provider's guidance diligently. If possible, discuss strategies to mitigate the impact on your gut flora, such as supplementing with probiotics during and after the antibiotic course.

- **Prebiotic-Rich Foods:** Include prebiotic-rich foods in your diet. Prebiotics are like fertilizers for beneficial bacteria. Foods like garlic, onions, bananas, and asparagus are excellent sources of prebiotics.
- **Stress Management:** Incorporate stress-reducing practices into your routine. Chronic stress can negatively impact gut flora. Techniques such as meditation, deep breathing exercises, and regular physical activity can support a healthier gut environment.
- **Gradual Changes:** Make changes slowly and observe how your body responds. Sudden and drastic shifts in diet can sometimes cause discomfort. Gradual adjustments allow your gut flora to adapt and thrive.

The Long-Term Benefits:

Committing to the slow and intentional repopulation of your gut flora yields enduring benefits. As your internal garden flourishes, you may experience improved digestion, enhanced nutrient absorption, and even notice positive effects on your mood and immune function. The journey to a resilient gut is not a quick fix but a sustained investment in your overall health and vitality. In cultivating a thriving gut flora, envision yourself as a gardener tending to the delicate balance within. Slowly and consciously, you nurture the diverse inhabitants of your gut, creating a resilient and flourishing ecosystem that contributes to your well-being.

3
CHAPTER
The Indian
Probiotic Rich
Diet

Introduction To Fermented Foods

1. Definition and Significance of Fermented Foods:

Fermentation is a time-honored metabolic process in which microorganisms, such as bacteria, yeast, or molds, break down carbohydrates in food into simpler compounds. This transformative process not only enhances the nutritional content of the food but also contributes unique flavors and textures. Foods that have undergone fermentation are known as fermented foods, and they are found in diverse culinary traditions worldwide. Examples include yogurt, kimchi, sauerkraut, and miso.

Fermented foods play a significant role in promoting gut health. The microorganisms involved in the fermentation process, often lactic acid bacteria, produce beneficial compounds like probiotics, which contribute to a healthy gut microbiome. Probiotics have been associated with various health benefits, including improved digestion, enhanced nutrient absorption, and strengthened immune function. Additionally, fermentation can increase the bioavailability of certain nutrients, making them more easily absorbed by the body.

Moreover, the impact of fermentation extends beyond mere nutritional enhancement, resonating profoundly with individuals facing common health challenges. For those familiar with feelings of bloating, gassiness, low energy, and a weakened immune system, the incorporation of fermented foods into one's diet becomes particularly relevant. Fermented foods

have been recognized for their potential to alleviate digestive discomfort by fostering a balanced gut microbiome. The probiotics generated through the fermentation process aid in regulating digestive processes, reducing sensations of bloating, and mitigating gassiness. Furthermore, the symbiotic relationship between fermented foods and immune health is increasingly acknowledged, with probiotics playing a role in fortifying the immune system. As we delve into the world of fermented Indian cuisine, it becomes apparent that the cultural embrace of these probiotic-rich delights not only enhances culinary experiences but also holds the promise of addressing common health concerns, contributing to overall well-being.

2. Historical Context of Fermentation in Indian Cuisine:

The use of fermentation in Indian cuisine has a deep-rooted historical context, dating back thousands of years. Various regions in India have practiced unique fermentation techniques, contributing to the diverse and flavorful array of traditional foods. One notable example is the fermentation of dosa and idli batter, a practice that originated in South India. This fermentation process involves naturally occurring microorganisms, resulting in the characteristic taste and texture of these popular dishes. Additionally, the art of pickling and fermenting vegetables and fruits has been a staple in Indian households for generations. This practice not only serves as a means of preserving seasonal produce but also introduces a spectrum of flavors to the Indian culinary landscape. Historical records and culinary texts reflect the significance of fermented foods in ancient Indian cultures, where the preservation and enhancement of food through fermentation were valued skills.

3. Brief Overview of the Fermentation Process:

The fermentation process involves the conversion of complex compounds, such as sugars and starches, into simpler substances through the action of microorganisms. In the context of Indian cuisine, this process is integral to the preparation of various staple foods. For instance, the fermentation of curd (yogurt) involves lactic acid bacteria, which not only preserve the dairy product but also contribute to its tangy flavor. Similarly, dosa and idli batter undergo fermentation, resulting in the characteristic light and fluffy texture of these South Indian delicacies.

Understanding the microbial involvement in fermentation is crucial. Lactic acid bacteria, commonly present in many fermented foods, produce organic acids and other bioactive compounds during the fermentation process. These compounds not only contribute to the unique flavors but also act as natural preservatives, extending the shelf life of the fermented products.

Prebiotic And Probiotic Concepts: Enhancing Gut Health

1. Understanding Prebiotics and their Role in Promoting Gut Health:

Prebiotics are a type of non-digestible fiber found in certain foods that nourish and stimulate the growth and activity of beneficial bacteria in the gut. Unlike probiotics, which are live beneficial bacteria, prebiotics serve as food for these bacteria, promoting a healthy and balanced gut microbiome. The gut microbiome refers to the trillions of microorganisms residing in the digestive tract, playing a crucial role in various aspects of health.

One prominent example of a prebiotic is inulin, found in foods like bananas, garlic, onions, and asparagus. When consumed, prebiotics pass through the stomach undigested and reach the colon, where they are fermented by the gut bacteria. This fermentation process produces short-chain fatty acids, which provide energy for the cells lining the colon and contribute to a well-nourished gut environment.

2. Exploring Probiotics and their Benefits for Digestion:

Probiotics are live microorganisms, mainly bacteria and yeast that confer health benefits to the host when consumed in adequate amounts. These microorganisms colonize the gut and contribute to the maintenance of a balanced and diverse gut microbiome. The digestive system is a complex environment with a delicate balance of various microorganisms. Factors such as antibiotic use, illness, or a poor diet can disrupt this balance, leading to digestive issues.

Probiotics help restore and maintain this balance by promoting the growth of beneficial bacteria. They enhance digestion by aiding in the breakdown of certain substances, producing essential nutrients, and preventing the overgrowth of harmful bacteria. Yogurt, kefir, sauerkraut, and kimchi are examples of foods rich in probiotics. Probiotic supplements are also available for those looking to boost their probiotic intake.

3. Synergy between Prebiotics and Probiotics:

The relationship between prebiotics and probiotics is symbiotic, creating a synergistic effect that significantly benefits gut health. Prebiotics act as the fuel for probiotics, helping them thrive and exert their positive effects in the digestive system. While probiotics introduce beneficial bacteria into the gut, prebiotics provide the necessary sustenance for these bacteria to flourish. This synergy enhances the overall effectiveness of the gut microbiome in supporting digestion, nutrient absorption, and immune function. Combining prebiotic-rich foods with probiotic sources creates an optimal environment for the growth of beneficial bacteria. For instance, consuming yogurt with added prebiotics or incorporating a variety of fiber-rich vegetables with fermented foods can maximize the synergistic effects of prebiotics and probiotics.

Understanding this synergy is crucial for individuals aiming to optimize their gut health. Including a diverse range of prebiotic and probiotic foods in the diet fosters a balanced and resilient gut micro biome, which is linked to improved overall health and well-being.

Culinary Journey Indian into Fermented Delicacies

In the realm of culinary traditions, Indian cuisine stands out not only for its vibrant array of flavors but also for its rich history of incorporating fermented foods that harness the power of probiotics. Fermentation, a time-honored technique, has been an integral part of Indian gastronomy for centuries, contributing not only to the preservation of food but also to the enhancement of taste and nutritional value. The art of fermenting ingredients such as rice, lentils, and vegetables has given rise to a diverse range of fermented delights like dosa, idli, and pickles, which are not only celebrated for their exquisite taste but also revered for their potential health benefits. These fermented treasures play a crucial role in promoting gut health by introducing beneficial bacteria, or probiotics, into the digestive system, adding an extra layer of significance to the tapestry of Indian culinary heritage.

1. Curd (Yogurt):

Traditional Methods of Curd Preparation:

Curd, a staple in Indian households, is often made through traditional methods that have been passed down through generations. The process typically involves inoculating milk with a small amount of previously fermented curd, allowing the natural bacteria in the curd to multiply and ferment the milk. This fermentation results in the thick and creamy texture characteristic of curd. The use of clay pots for fermentation is a traditional practice, as they provide an ideal environment for the growth of beneficial bacteria.

Nutritional Benefits of Curd Consumption:

Curd is not only a delicious addition to meals but also offers numerous nutritional benefits. It is an excellent source of calcium, essential for bone health, and is rich in protein, promoting muscle development and repair. Additionally, curd contains probiotics, live beneficial bacteria that support gut health. The probiotics in curd contribute to a balanced gut microbiome, aiding in digestion and boosting the immune system.

Varieties of Curd and Their Regional Variations:

The diversity of Indian culture is reflected in the various regional variations of curd. In North India, "Dahi" is a popular form of curd, often enjoyed with meals or used to make refreshing drinks like lassi. In South India, "Thayir" is a common term for curd, and it plays a crucial role in the preparation of dishes like curd rice. Regional variations also extend to the use of different milk sources, such as buffalo milk for a creamier texture in some northern regions. Each variation offers a unique flavor profile, showcasing the culinary richness of the country.

Gut Health and Curd: A Probiotic Powerhouse

Gut health is a crucial aspect of overall well-being, influencing digestion, immune function, and even mental health. Probiotics often referred to as "good" or "friendly" bacteria play a pivotal role in maintaining a balanced and healthy gut microbiome. Curd, a staple in many cultures, stands out as a probiotic powerhouse, contributing to improved gut health. Curd is rich in probiotics, primarily lactic acid bacteria, which are essential for promoting a flourishing gut microbiota. These live microorganisms act as reinforcements for the existing beneficial bacteria in the digestive system, fostering a diverse and resilient microbial environment. The probiotics in curd help maintain the delicate balance between good and bad bacteria in the gut, contributing to optimal digestive function.

Consuming curd regularly can aid in various aspects of gut health. Probiotics enhance the digestion and absorption of nutrients, promoting better nutrient utilization. Additionally, they play a role in preventing the overgrowth of harmful bacteria, reducing the risk of digestive issues such as bloating, constipation, and irritable bowel syndrome. Furthermore, the benefits of curd extend beyond the digestive system. Probiotics in curd have been associated with improved immune function, potentially reducing the susceptibility to infections. Some studies even suggest a connection between a healthy gut microbiome, influenced by probiotic-rich foods like curd, and mental well-being, highlighting the intricate gut-brain connection. Incorporating curd into the daily diet, whether consumed on its own, in smoothies, or as part of savory dishes, provides a tasty and accessible way to support gut health. However, it's essential to choose plain, unsweetened curd with live cultures for maximum probiotic benefits. As a versatile and culturally significant food, curd stands as a delicious ally in nurturing and maintaining a healthy gut, contributing to overall vitality and wellness.

2. Chaas (Buttermilk): A Refreshing Elixir of Health And Tradition

Making Chaas at Home:

Chaas, also known as buttermilk, is a delightful and refreshing beverage deeply rooted in Indian culinary traditions. Making chaas at home is a simple and rewarding process. Start with fresh yogurt, preferably homemade, and dilute it with water to achieve the desired consistency. The mixture is then seasoned with an array of aromatic spices, typically including roasted cumin powder, salt, and sometimes a hint of mint or coriander. This concoction is traditionally churned to enhance the frothy texture and amalgamate the flavors. However, a simple whisk or blender can also be used for convenience. The art of making chaas at home is not just about crafting a drink; it's a connection to heritage and a celebration of regional diversity. Families often pass down unique chaas recipes, each with its distinctive combination of spices, making it a personal and cherished element of Indian households.

Health Benefits of Including Buttermilk in the Diet:

Beyond its delightful taste, chaas offers an array of health benefits, making it a valuable addition to one's diet. First and foremost, buttermilk is a probiotic-rich beverage. The live cultures present in yogurt used to make chaas are beneficial bacteria that support a healthy gut microbiome. These probiotics aid in digestion, improve nutrient absorption, and contribute to overall gut health.Moreover, buttermilk is a low-calorie drink, making it an excellent choice for those aiming to maintain or lose weight. It provides a sense of fullness without the added calories, making it a satisfying and guilt-free option for those between meals or as a light snack.

The incorporation of spices in chaas is not just for flavor; it also adds a nutritional dimension. Roasted cumin, for example, not only enhances the aroma but also brings digestive benefits. Cumin is believed to aid in digestion, reduce bloating, and alleviate indigestion. This combination of probiotics and digestive spices positions chaas as a holistic digestive aid, contributing to overall gastrointestinal wellness.

Chaas Recipes and Variations:

While the basic chaas recipe forms the foundation, the beauty lies in its versatility. Chaas can be tailored to suit individual preferences, and regional variations abound. Some regions prefer a spicier version, incorporating green chilies, ginger, and asafoetida. Others may opt for a sweeter profile with the addition of sugar or jaggery.

a. Mint Chaas Recipe

Ingredients:

- 1 cup fresh yogurt
- 1 cup water
- 1/2 teaspoon roasted cumin powder
- Salt to taste
- A handful of fresh mint leaves
- Ice cubes (optional)

Instructions:

1. In a blender, combine yogurt, water, roasted cumin powder, salt, and mint leaves.
2. Blend until smooth.
3. Strain the mixture to remove mint leaves if desired.
4. Serve over ice for a refreshing twist.

b. Spicy Masala Chaas Recipe

Ingredients:

- 1 cup fresh yogurt
- 1 cup water
- 1/2 teaspoon roasted cumin powder
- Salt to taste
- 1/4 teaspoon black salt
- 1/4 teaspoon chaat masala
- 1/4 teaspoon black pepper
- Fresh coriander leaves for garnish

Instructions:

1. In a blender, combine yogurt, water, roasted cumin powder, salt, black salt, chaat masala, and black pepper.
2. Blend until well combined.
3. Garnish with fresh coriander leaves.
4. Serve chilled.

These recipes showcase the adaptability of chaas, inviting individuals to experiment with flavors and tailor the beverage to their liking. The addition of fresh herbs, spices, or even seasonal fruits can elevate the experience, transforming chaas into a versatile and enjoyable drink for any occasion.

3. Lassi: Different Types, Refreshing Beverage, And Cultural Contexts

Different Types of Lassi (Sweet, Salty, Fruity):

Lassi, another iconic Indian yogurt-based beverage, stands as a testament to the country's culinary diversity. This versatile drink comes in various types, each offering a unique flavor profile.

Sweet Lassi: This rendition involves blending yogurt with water, sugar, and sometimes fruit like mango, creating a sweet and indulgent concoction. It is a delightful way to satisfy a sweet tooth, especially during the scorching summer months.

Salty Lassi: In contrast, salty lassi incorporates salt, cumin, and other savory spices. This version is a savory counterpart to the sweet variant, offering a refreshing and mildly spiced alternative. It is particularly favored as a cooling beverage to complement spicy meals.

Fruity Lassi: Adding a fruity twist to lassi involves blending yogurt with fresh fruits like mango, strawberry, or banana. This variation not only enhances the natural sweetness but also introduces additional vitamins and minerals.

Lassi as a Refreshing Beverage:

Lassi, in all its variations, stands out as a quint essential Indian refreshment, especially during the sweltering summer months. The cool, yogurt-based drink provides instant relief from the heat and replenishes essential electrolytes. The balance of yogurt and water in lassi makes it a hydrating choice, ensuring a refreshing experience with every sip. Beyond its cooling properties, lassi offers nutritional benefits. Yogurt, the main ingredient in lassi, is a rich source of protein, calcium, and probiotics. The probiotics contribute to gut health, promoting a diverse and thriving microbiome.

Lassi in Indian Cultural Contexts:

Lassi is not merely a beverage; it's a cultural phenomenon deeply woven into the fabric of Indian traditions. Its roots trace back centuries, with mentions in ancient Ayurvedic texts as a digestive aid. The versatility of lassi allows it to transcend regional boundaries, adapting to local flavors and preferences. During festivals and celebrations, lassi takes on a ceremonial role. Sweet lassi may be offered as a symbol of hospitality and celebration, while salty lassi serves as a palate cleanser between festive meals. In Punjab, the land of the Bhangra and vibrant culture, festivals witness the preparation of a unique version called "Bhang Lassi," infused with cannabis for ceremonial (Holi) consumption. The cultural significance of lassi extends beyond its role as a beverage. It embodies the spirit of sharing, community, and joy, making it an integral part of gatherings, whether in bustling markets or serene family dinners.

4. Kanji (Kanji Recipes): A Cultural Tapestry of Fermented Elixirs

Introduction to Kanji and its Cultural Significance:

Kanji, a traditional Indian fermented beverage, weaves a rich tapestry of cultural significance, rooted in centuries-old culinary practices. The word "Kanji" finds its origin in the Sanskrit language, meaning 'fermented water.' This traditional drink holds a special place in Indian households, especially during festivals like Holi. The cultural significance of Kanji extends beyond its ingredients. It is deeply ingrained in festive traditions and often associated with rituals of cleansing and renewal. The preparation of Kanji traditionally begins a few days before Holi, marking the arrival of spring. The festival is not only a celebration of colors but also a time for rejuvenation and the ushering in of new beginnings. Kanji, with its fermentation process and unique flavor profile, mirrors this spirit of transformation and regeneration. In the cultural landscape of North India, particularly in states like Rajasthan, Kanji is more than just a beverage; it is a symbol of community, tradition, and the vibrant tapestry of Indian festivals

Variations of Kanji Recipes from Different Regions:

The beauty of Kanji lies in its adaptability with disparities spanning different regions. Each adds its unique twist to the traditional recipe.

Classic Kanji Recipe

Ingredients:

- Black carrots
- Mustard seeds
- Rock salt
- Water

Instructions:

1. Wash and peel the black carrots.
2. Cut the carrots into thin, uniform sticks.
3. In a glass jar, layer the carrot sticks with mustard seeds and rock salt.
4. Fill the jar with water, ensuring that the carrots are fully submerged.
5. Seal the jar and place it in a sunny spot for fermentation.
6. After 3-4 days, the Kanji is ready to be consumed.

Variations:

Spiced Kanji: Some regions enhance the spiciness by adding red chili powder, ginger, and turmeric. These additions not only infuse a deeper flavor but also contribute to the health benefits associated with these spices.

Mixed Vegetable Kanji: In some households, a medley of vegetables like beets, turnips, and radishes are included, creating a colorful and nutritious concoction.

Sweet Kanji: A departure from the traditional savory version, sweet Kanji involves the addition of jaggery or sugar, providing a delightful contrast to the tangy and spicy undertones.

Fruity Kanji: Embracing the diversity of Indian fruits, some variations include the infusion of fruits like apples or pears, adding a refreshing and sweet element to the fermented drink.

These regional variations showcase the adaptability of Kanji, allowing individuals to tailor the beverage to their taste preferences and local ingredients. Each version reflects the unique culinary identity of its region, contributing to the diverse gastronomic landscape of India.

Health Benefits of Consuming Kanji:

The consumption of Kanji goes beyond its cultural significance; it offers a spectrum of health benefits, thanks to the fermentation process and the natural components of its ingredients.

a. Probiotic Richness: The fermentation of Kanji involves the proliferation of beneficial bacteria, transforming it into a probiotic-rich beverage. Lactic acid bacterium a natural byproduct of fermentation, populate the drink and contributes to a healthy gut microbiome. Probiotics are known for their role in supporting digestion, enhancing nutrient absorption, and bolstering the immune system.	**b. Nutrient Boost:** The primary ingredient in Kanji, black carrots, is a nutritional powerhouse. These carrots are rich in antioxidants, particularly anthocyanins, which contribute to their deep purple color. Anthocyanins have been linked to various health benefits, including anti-inflammatory and cardiovascular protective effects.
d. Digestive Aid: Mustard seeds, a common component in Kanji, bring a pungent flavor and a host of health benefits. They are known for their digestive properties, aiding in the breakdown of food and promoting overall digestive wellness. Mustard seeds also contain compounds with anti-inflammatory and antimicrobial properties.	**c. Electrolyte Balance:** The inclusion of rock salt in Kanji not only adds to its distinct taste but also provides essential minerals. The balanced presence of sodium and potassium helps maintain electrolyte balance, crucial for hydration and various physiological functions.
e. Detoxification: The fermentation process in Kanji not only enhances flavor but also contributes to the detoxification of the body. Fermented foods have been associated with promoting the elimination of toxins and supporting the liver's natural detoxification processes.	

5. Fermented Pickles: Traditional Methods, Probiotic Content, And Regional Recipes

Traditional Methods of Pickling in India:

Pickling in India is an age-old culinary practice that serves not only as a method of preserving seasonal produce but also as a wa+6y to infuse unique flavors into everyday meals. The traditional methods of pickling vary across regions but share common principles.

Basic Steps for Pickling:

i. Selection of Vegetables: Vegetables like mangoes, lime, green chilies, and even certain roots are chosen for pickling based on their texture and taste.	**ii Brining:** Vegetables are often soaked in a brine solution, typically consisting of salt and sometimes turmeric, for a few hours. This step not only seasons the vegetables but also draws out excess moisture, aiding in the preservation process.
iii. Spicing: The brined vegetables are then mixed with an array of spices, including mustard seeds, fenugreek seeds, asafoetida, and red chili powder. The combination of these spices contributes to the unique and bold flavors associated with Indian pickles.	**iv. Oil Infusion:** Some pickles involve the addition of mustard oil, which not only acts as a preservative but also imparts a distinct taste. Mustard oil is heated with spices to create infused oil that is then poured over the prepared vegetables.
v. Sun-Drying: The pickles are often sun-dried for a few days, allowing the flavors to intensify and aiding in the preservation process. The exposure to sunlight also acts as a natural antimicrobial, further enhancing the shelf life of the pickles.	

Probiotic Content in Fermented Pickles:

The magic of Indian pickles lies not just in their taste but also in their probiotic content. The fermentation process, coupled with the presence of various spices, creates an environment conducive to the growth of beneficial bacteria. Lactic acid bacteria, the heroes of fermentation, are responsible for the tangy flavor and contribute to the probiotic richness of pickles.

Popular Regional Pickle Recipes:

a. Mango Pickle (Aam ka Achaar): Perhaps the most iconic of all Indian pickles, mango pickle is a culinary masterpiece enjoyed across the country. Raw mangoes are cut into pieces and marinated with a blend of mustard seeds, fenugreek seeds, red chili powder, asafoetida, and salt. The mixture is then submerged in mustard oil, creating a pickle that tantalizes the taste buds with its combination of sweet, sour, and spicy notes.	**b. Lime Pickle (Nimbu ka Achaar):** Lime pickle is a zesty creation that involves marinating lime wedges with salt and chili powder. Mustard seeds and fenugreek seeds add depth, while the infusion of mustard oil completes the flavorful medley. Lime pickle is a staple accompaniment to Indian meals, providing a burst of tanginess.

c. Green Chili Pickle (Mirchi ka Achaar): For those seeking an extra kick, green chili pickle delivers a fiery punch. Green chilies are slit and stuffed with a mixture of spices, including mustard seeds, fenugreek seeds, asafoetida, and salt. The pickling process transforms the intense heat of the chilies into a flavorful spiciness that pairs well with various dishes.

d. Mixed Vegetable Pickle: This medley of vegetables, including carrots, cauliflower, and turnips, showcases the diversity of Indian pickles. The vegetables are chopped, brined, and seasoned with a blend of spices before being immersed in mustard oil. The result is a colorful and crunchy pickle that adds texture and flavor to any meal.

e. Garlic Pickle (Lehsun ka Achaar): Garlic lovers rejoice in the pungent delight of garlic pickle. Whole garlic cloves are pickled with mustard seeds, red chili powder, and salt. The intensity of the garlic combines with the spices to create a robust pickle that elevates the simplest of dishes.

These regional pickle recipes exemplify the culinary prowess embedded in Indian households. Each pickle carries a story of tradition, innovation, and the distinct flavors of its region.

6. Fermented Pulses And Rice: A Culinary Symphony Of Tradition And Nutrition

Fermentation has been an integral part of Indian cuisine for centuries, contributing not only to the preservation of food but also to the creation of unique flavors and enhanced nutritional profiles. In the realm of fermented foods, pulses and rice take center stage, offering a delightful array of dishes that resonate with cultural richness and health benefits.

Fermented Lentils and Pulses in Indian Cuisine:

In the vast tapestry of Indian cuisine, lentils and pulses hold a revered position, serving as primary sources of protein for a predominantly vegetarian population. The process of fermenting these pulses not only elevates their nutritional value but also imparts a distinct taste and texture to the dishes. One of the quintessential fermented pulse dishes is "Dal Dhokli," originating from the western state of Gujarat. This dish involves fermenting a mixture of lentils, predominantly tuvar dal, overnight. The fermentation not only aids in digestion but also enhances the flavor profile, creating a harmonious blend of tanginess and earthiness.

The fermentation process begins with soaking the lentils in water, allowing them to sprout. The sprouting process not only enhances the nutritional content by breaking down complex compounds but also initiates the production of enzymes that aid in digestion. The soaked lentils are then ground into a batter, mixed with spices, and left to ferment. The result is a fermented lentil batter that forms the base for various dishes, including dhokli, dosa, and idli.

VINDHYA SINGH

Rice-Based Fermented Dishes:

Rice, another staple in Indian cuisine, undergoes a transformative journey through the process of fermentation, giving rise to beloved dishes like idli and dosa. The synergy between rice and pulses in these fermented creations not only contributes to their unique textures but also forms a complementary protein source.

a.   Idli and Dosa Batter:

The iconic idli and dosa, popular across India and beyond, are made from a batter of fermented rice and urad dal (black gram). The fermentation process is a crucial step that not only imparts a distinct taste but also enhances the nutritional value of these dishes. To prepare the batter, rice and urad dal are soaked separately before being ground into a fine paste. The two pastes are then mixed in the correct proportion, creating a batter that is left to ferment overnight. The natural microorganisms present in the environment and the ingredients initiate the fermentation, resulting in the characteristic texture and taste of idli and dosa.

The fermentation process in idli and dosa batter not only breaks down complex carbohydrates but also increases the bioavailability of nutrients. The beneficial bacteria produced during fermentation contribute to the probiotic content of these dishes, supporting gut health. The result is a light, fluffy idli with a subtle tanginess and crispy dosa with a delightful golden-brown hue.

Nutritional Value and Preparation Methods:

The nutritional value of fermented pulses and rice-based dishes is a testament to the health benefits embedded in traditional Indian fare.

i. Bioavailability of Nutrients: Fermentation transforms the nutritional composition of pulses and rice, making the nutrients more easily absorbable by the body. The process breaks down anti-nutrients, such as phytates and tannins that can interfere with the absorption of minerals like iron and zinc. The increased bioavailability of nutrients makes these fermented dishes not only delicious but also nutritious.	**ii. Probiotic Content:** The fermentation process introduces beneficial bacteria, primarily lactic acid bacteria, into these dishes. These probiotics contribute to a healthy gut microbiome, supporting digestion and overall gut health. Studies have shown that fermented foods play a role in maintaining a balanced gut microbiota, which is linked to various aspects of health, including immune function and mental well-being.

iii. Balanced Protein Source: Combination of pulses and rice in fermented dishes creates a balanced protein source. Pulses are rich in essential amino acids, and when paired with rice, which provides complementary amino acids, the result is a complete protein profile. This is particularly

crucial in vegetarian diets, where obtaining all essential amino acids can be a challenge. Fermented pulses and rice dishes not only celebrate the diversity of Indian cuisine but also offer a window into the intricate relationship between traditional practices and modern nutritional understanding. As we savor these fermented delights, we not only indulge our taste buds but also partake in a culinary heritage that spans generations, nourishing both body and soul.

Gut Health and the Nurturing Power of Fermented Rice and Pulses

Gut health is a cornerstone of overall well-being, influencing digestion, immune function, and even mental health. In the culinary landscape of India, fermented rice and pulses play a pivotal role in not just satiating the palate but also in nurturing a healthy gut microbiome.

Fermented Rice and Pulses: Guardians of Gut Health:

Fermented Rice:

In the realm of fermented rice, the spotlight shines brightly on iconic dishes like idli and dosa. These South Indian delicacies, born from the alchemy of rice and urad dal fermentation, are not just culinary delights but also allies in promoting gut health.

a. Probiotic Richness: The fermentation process in idli and dosa batter is orchestrated by the natural interplay of microorganisms present in the environment and the ingredients. This gives rise to probiotics, specifically lactic acid bacteria, which are known for their beneficial role in gut health. Probiotics contribute to a diverse and balanced gut microbiome, fostering an environment that supports optimal digestion and nutrient absorption.	**b. Digestive Wellness:** Fermented rice aids in breaking down complex carbohydrates into simpler forms, making nutrients more accessible to the body. This process not only enhances the bioavailability of nutrients but also promotes easier digestion. For individuals with sensitivities or mild digestive issues, incorporating fermented rice dishes into the diet can be a gentle and flavorful way to support digestive wellness.

Fermented Pulses

Lentils and pulses, foundational elements in Indian cuisine, undergo a transformative journey through fermentation, contributing to both flavor complexity and gut health.

a. Prebiotics in Pulses: Pulses, even before fermentation, are rich in prebiotics – non-digestible fibers that serve as food for beneficial gut bacteria. These prebiotics act as a	**b. Protein Digestion:** Fermentation of pulses initiates the breakdown of complex proteins into more digestible forms. This can be particularly beneficial for individuals who may

nourishing substrate for the existing microbial community in the gut, promoting the growth of beneficial bacteria.	experience discomfort or bloating after consuming certain protein-rich foods. The fermentation process begins the pre-digestion of proteins, potentially making them easier on the digestive system.

The Synergy of Probiotics and Prebiotics:

The combination of fermented rice and pulses in dishes like idli and dosa creates a powerful synergy between probiotics and prebiotics, fostering a balanced gut environment.

a. Probiotics from Fermented Rice: The probiotics generated during the fermentation of rice complement the prebiotics naturally present in pulses. This synergistic relationship promotes the growth and activity of beneficial bacteria in the gut.	**b. Comprehensive Gut Support:** While probiotics contribute to the introduction of beneficial bacteria, prebiotics act as fuel for these microorganisms, ensuring their sustained presence and activity in the gut. This comprehensive support is crucial for maintaining a resilient and balanced gut microbiome.

As we savor the delights of fermented rice and pulses, we embark on a culinary journey that not only delights the taste buds but also nourishes the intricate ecosystem within our digestive tract. In the harmony of probiotics and prebiotics, these traditional dishes emerge as guardians of gut health, inviting us to embrace the rich tapestry of flavors while caring for our well-being.

7. The Fermented Magic of Idli and Dosa Batter: A Nutritional Odyssey

In the vibrant mosaic of Indian cuisine, idli and dosa stand as timeless classics, revered not only for their culinary excellence but also for their profound impact on health. At the heart of these delectable creations lies the alchemy of fermented batter, a process that transforms humble rice and pulses into a nutritional powerhouse. As we delve into the world of idli and dosa batter, we uncover not just the secrets of their preparation but also their potential to shape the future of healthy eating.

Fermentation Process in Idli and Dosa Batter:

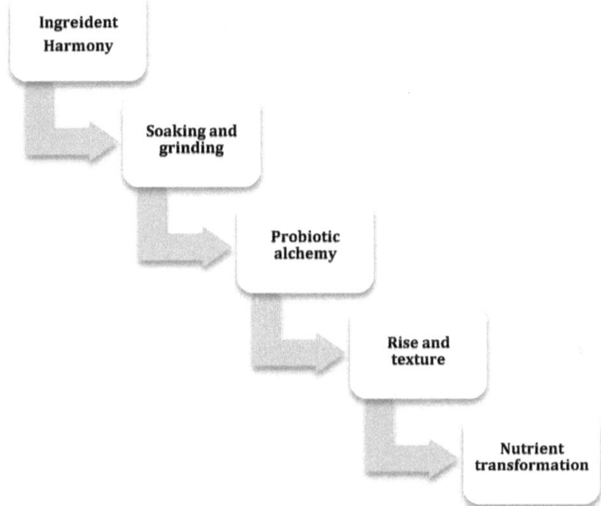

The journey from raw ingredients to the softness of idlis and the crispiness of dosas is orchestrated by the transformative process of fermentation. This natural and age-old technique not only imparts the characteristic taste and texture to these dishes but also significantly enhances their nutritional profile.

i. Ingredient Harmony: The foundation of idli and dosa batter lies in the harmonious blend of rice and urad dal (black gram). The proportion and quality of these ingredients play a crucial role in the success of the fermentation process. Rice provides the bulk of the batter, contributing to the texture, while urad dal adds a rich source of protein.	**ii. Soaking and Grinding:** The journey begins with soaking the rice and urad dal separately. This soaking process initiates several biochemical reactions, including the activation of enzymes and the breakdown of complex compounds. After soaking, the ingredients are ground into a smooth batter, often with the addition of fenugreek seeds to aid fermentation.

<table>
<tr>
<td>

iii. Probiotic Alchemy: Once ground, the batter is left to undergo the magic of fermentation. The natural microorganisms present in the environment and the ingredients, along with the enzymes activated during soaking, initiate a complex dance of biochemical reactions. The star players in this process are lactic acid bacteria, which thrive in the batter, producing lactic acid and carbon dioxide.

</td>
<td>

iv. Rise and Texture: As the bacteria work their magic, carbon dioxide is released, causing the batter to rise and become airy. This results in the characteristic sponginess of idlis and the porous texture of dosas. The longer the fermentation, the more pronounced the tangy flavor and softer the texture, creating a perfect symphony of taste and mouthfeel.

</td>
</tr>
<tr>
<td colspan="2">

iv. Nutrient Transformation: Beyond the sensory delights, fermentation significantly transforms the nutritional composition of the batter. Complex carbohydrates are broken down into simpler forms, making them easier to digest. The probiotics generated during fermentation contribute to the gut-friendly nature of these dishes.

</td>
</tr>
</table>

Idli and Dosa Variations

While the traditional idli and dosa hold a special place in the culinary repertoire, the versatility of the fermented batter opens the door to a myriad of variations, each offering a unique culinary experience.

Classic Idli

The iconic idli, with its soft and fluffy texture, is a breakfast favorite across India. Served with coconut chutney and sambar, it embodies the perfect balance of taste and nutrition. The fermentation process ensures that the idlis are not just a delightful culinary experience but also a probiotic-rich start to the day.

<table>
<tr>
<td>

a. Masala Dosa

Dosa, a thin and crispy cousin of idli, takes on various forms. The masala dosa, filled with a spiced potato mixture, is a hearty and satisfying meal. The dosa batter, with its tangy undertones from fermentation, complements the earthy flavors of the potato filling, creating a symphony of tastes and textures.

</td>
<td>

b. Rava Dosa

Rava dosa introduces semolina into the batter, adding a delightful crunch to the dosa. The fermentation process still plays a crucial role, contributing to the distinctive flavor and the porous structure that allows the batter to crisp up beautifully when cooked.

</td>
</tr>
</table>

c. **Uthappam**	d. **Pesarattu**
Uthappam, a thicker cousin of dosa, incorporates a variety of toppings, including onions, tomatoes, and chilies. The fermented batter forms the base, providing the characteristic tanginess and a soft interior beneath the flavorful toppings	Hailing from the southern state of Andhra Pradesh, pesarattu is a dosa made from green gram (moong dal). The batter, fermented to perfection, brings a unique flavor and nutritional boost to this protein-rich dish.

Breakfast and Snack Ideas Using Fermented Batters:

The versatility of idli and dosa batter extends beyond the realms of breakfast, offering a canvas for culinary creativity throughout the day

- **Idli Chaat:** Transform leftover idlis into a delightful chaat by cutting them into bite-sized pieces and topping them with a medley of chopped vegetables, chutneys, and spices. This fusion dish combines the wholesome goodness of idlis with the vibrant flavors of chaat.

- **Dosa Rolls:** Roll up dosas with a variety of fillings to create a portable and satisfying snack. Whether filled with spiced potatoes, paneer, or even leftover stir-fried vegetables, dosa rolls are a versatile and delicious option for on-the-go eating.

- **Mini Uttapams:** Use the fermented batter to create bite-sized uttapams, each topped with a different combination of vegetables and cheese. These mini delights are perfect for entertaining or as a creative snack for kids.

- **Dosa Wraps:** Fill dosas with a mix of fresh vegetables, hummus, and a protein source like grilled chicken or tofu to create wholesome and flavorful wraps. The tangy notes from the fermented batter add an extra dimension to the overall taste.

- **Instant Rava Idli:** For a quick and nutritious variation, mix semolina (rava) with yogurt and spices to create an instant idli batter. While not fermented, this quick version still provides a tasty and healthier alternative to traditional instant foods.

Health Benefits of Idli and Its Importance in the Future:

The health benefits of idli extend far beyond its role as a beloved breakfast item. As we look towards the future of food and nutrition, idli emerges as a symbol of balance, combining culinary tradition with modern health-conscious sensibilities.

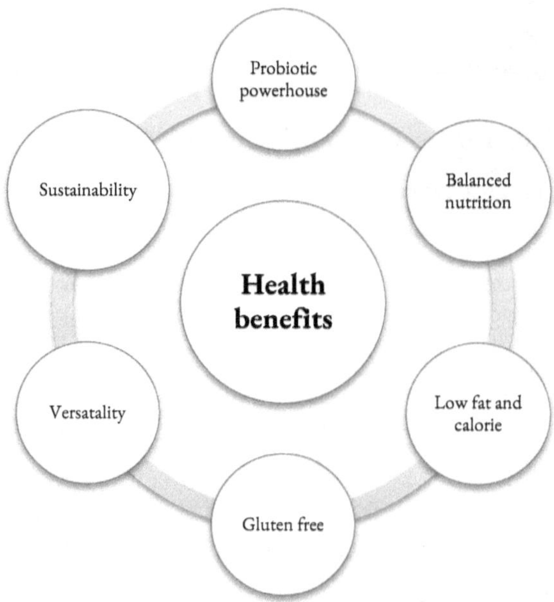

i. **Probiotic Powerhouse:** The fermentation process in idli batter introduces probiotics, specifically lactic acid bacteria, which contribute to a healthy gut microbiome. As the scientific community delves deeper into the intricacies of gut health and its impact on overall well-being, the probiotic-rich nature of idlis positions them as a valuable addition to a diet that prioritizes digestive wellness.

ii. **Balanced Nutrition:** The combination of rice and urad dal in idli batter creates a balanced source of protein. In a world where plant-based diets are gaining prominence, idlis provide a complete amino acid profile, addressing the nutritional needs of those opting for vegetarian or vegan lifestyles.

iii. **Low Fat and Calorie Content:** Idlis and dosas, when steamed or cooked on a non-stick surface without excessive oil, are inherently low in fat and calories. As the global focus on maintaining a healthy weight and preventing lifestyle-related diseases intensifies, idlis emerge as a satisfying and nutritious option.

iv. **Gluten-Free and Fermented Goodness:** With the rise in awareness of gluten sensitivity and the benefits of fermented foods, idlis fit seamlessly into gluten-free and gut-friendly diets. The fermentation process not only makes nutrients more accessible but also breaks down potential allergens present in grains, contributing to better digestibility.

v. **Versatility for Modern Lifestyles:** The adaptability of idli and dosa batter to various culinary creations aligns with the demands of modern lifestyles. From quick wraps to innovative snacks, idlis provide a canvas for creative and healthy eating, catering to individuals seeking convenient yet nourishing options.

vi. **Sustainable and Plant-Based:** As conversations around sustainable eating gain momentum, idlis showcase the potential of plant-based, locally sourced ingredients. The simplicity of rice and urad dal, coupled with the minimal environmental impact of fermentation, positions idlis as a sustainable and eco-friendly choice.

The Future of Idli in a Changing Culinary Landscape:

As we stand at the crossroads of culinary tradition and a rapidly evolving food landscape, the future of idli appears promising and influential. Here's why idli is poised to play a pivotal role in shaping the way we eat

❖ **Culinary Fusion and Innovation:** Idli's adaptability opens the door to endless culinary possibilities. Whether it's incorporating global flavors into idli variations or reimagining traditional dishes, the versatility of idlis allows for innovation and fusion, appealing to a diverse and evolving palate.

❖ **Nutrient-Dense Convenience:** In an era where convenience often comes at the cost of nutrition, idlis stand as a beacon of nutrient-dense convenience. The ease of preparing fermented batter in advance, coupled with the quick cooking time of idlis, aligns with the demands of busy lifestyles without compromising on health.

❖ **Global Acceptance:** With the increasing global appreciation for diverse cuisines, idlis are finding their way onto international menus. As a symbol of health and flavor, idlis have the potential to transcend cultural boundaries, introducing a broader audience to the benefits of fermented, plant-based nutrition.

In the grand tapestry of culinary delights, idli and dosa batter emerge not only as beloved dishes but as beacons of health and tradition. The fermentation process, a time-honored practice, weaves a story of probiotic richness, balanced nutrition, and culinary versatility. As we navigate the future of food, idlis stand as ambassadors of a holistic approach to eating—where flavor, tradition, and health converge to create a nourishing and delightful experience. In embracing idlis and dosas, we not only celebrate the heritage of Indian cuisine but also embrace a future where the intersection of culinary tradition and nutritional wisdom shapes a healthier, more vibrant world.

Idly: Wholesome Heritage, Tomorrow's Health on a Plate!

Vindhya Singh

8. Dhokla: A Culinary Tapestry Of Fermentation, Flavor, And Health

In the mixture of Indian cuisine, Dhokla stands out as a testament to the artistry of fermentation, where simplicity meets sophistication on a plate. Originating from the western Indian state of Gujarat, Dhokla has transcended regional borders to become a beloved dish across the country and beyond. As we embark on a journey into the world of Dhokla, we'll unravel the secrets of its fermentation process, explore the diverse types of Dhokla with regional specialties, and discover how this flavorful creation can be seamlessly incorporated into a balanced and health-conscious diet.

Fermentation in Dhokla Preparation

At the heart of Dhokla's unique texture and tangy flavor lies the transformative power of fermentation. This age-old culinary technique not only enhances the taste and aroma of the dish but also contributes to its nutritional profile.

a. Ingredients and Preparation: The key ingredients for Dhokla include fermented rice and chickpea flour (besan), which are combined with yogurt and a blend of spices. The fermentation process begins with mixing these ingredients into a batter, which is then left to ferment for several hours. The use of yogurt introduces lactic acid bacteria, which play a crucial role in the fermentation process.	**b. Probiotics in Dhokla:** The naturally occurring microorganisms in the environment, coupled with those present in the yogurt, initiate a cascade of biochemical reactions during fermentation. Lactic acid bacteria proliferate in the batter, producing lactic acid as a byproduct. This not only imparts the characteristic tanginess to Dhokla but also introduces probiotics – beneficial bacteria known for their positive impact on gut health.
c. Rise and Texture: As fermentation a progress, carbon dioxide is released, causing the batter to rise. The result is a spongy and light texture that defines Dhokla. The longer the fermentation, the more pronounced the tangy flavor and softer the texture, creating a delightful harmony of taste and mouth feel.	**d. Nutritional Benefits:** Beyond the sensory experience, the fermentation process in Dhokla brings forth nutritional benefits. The breakdown of complex carbohydrates makes the nutrients more easily absorbable, and the introduction of probiotics enhances the dish's gut-friendly properties.

Types of Dhokla and Their Regional Specialties:

Dhokla, a versatile dish, manifests in various forms across different regions of India, each with its unique characteristics and regional specialties.

❖ **Khaman Dhokla:** Originating from Gujarat, Khaman Dhokla is perhaps the most well-known variation. It is characterized by its soft and spongy texture, attributed to the fine balance of ingredients and the meticulous fermentation process. Typically served with green chutney and a sprinkle of grated coconut, Khaman Dhokla is a delightful snack or breakfast item.

- ❖ **Dhokla with Eno:** An innovation in Dhokla preparation involves the use of Eno, an antacid fruit salt, to expedite the fermentation process. This quick version of Dhokla is popular for its convenience, allowing for almost instant preparation. While purists may argue that the traditional fermentation method yields a superior texture and taste, the Eno-based Dhokla remains a quick and accessible option.

- ❖ **Rava Dhokla:** Rava Dhokla introduces semolina (sooji) into the batter, adding a grainy texture to the dish. The fermentation process still plays a crucial role, contributing to the distinctive flavor and the porous structure that allows the batter to absorb the accompanying tempering of mustard seeds, curry leaves, and green chilies.

- ❖ **Dhokla with Methi Leaves:** Incorporating fenugreek leaves (methi) into the batter not only infuses a unique flavor but also enhances the nutritional value of Dhokla. The bitterness of methi leaves balances the overall taste, creating a Dhokla variation that is both flavorful and nutritious.

- ❖ **Besan Dhokla:** Besan Dhokla, made primarily with chickpea flour, showcases a denser texture compared to its counterparts. The batter is typically flavored with spices like turmeric, red chili, and asafoetida, creating a vibrant and savory profile. This variation is often enjoyed as a snack or a side dish.

- ❖ **Dhokla Sandwich:** A creative twist on traditional Dhokla involves layering it with chutney and other fillings to create a sandwich. This fusion of flavors and textures adds a contemporary touch to the classic dish, making it suitable for a quick and satisfying meal.

Incorporating Dhokla into a Balanced Diet

Beyond its regional variations, Dhokla stands as a versatile and nutritious addition to a balanced diet. Here's how Dhokla can be seamlessly integrated into different meals:

- **Healthy Snacking:** Dhokla, with its balanced combination of protein from chickpea flour and probiotics from fermentation, makes for a healthy snacking option. Cut into bite-sized pieces and paired with a mint chutney or yogurt dip, Dhokla satisfies snack cravings without compromising on nutritional value.

- **Breakfast Bliss:** Dhokla, served alongside a refreshing cup of masala chai or as part of a larger breakfast spread, brings a wholesome start to the day. Its light yet filling nature makes it an excellent choice for those looking to kickstart their mornings with a nutritious and energizing meal.

- **Main Course Accompaniment:** Dhokla can be paired with a variety of main course dishes, complementing the flavors of curries, dals, or vegetable preparations. Its ability to absorb the essence of accompanying gravies and spices makes Dhokla a versatile addition to lunch or dinner.

- **Healthy Side Dish:** Replace traditional bread or rice with Dhokla as a side dish. Its probiotic content and low-fat profile contribute to a well-rounded and healthy meal, especially when paired with fiber-rich vegetables and lean protein sources.

- **Innovative Appetizers:** Dhokla's adaptable nature allows for creative appetizer presentations. Whether served as Dhokla skewers with colorful veggies or as a base for miniature sliders, its mild yet flavorful taste provides a canvas for culinary innovation.

9. Fermented Vegetables: Krauts, Kimchi

As we transition from the Indian subcontinent to the global realm of fermented vegetables, Krauts and Kimchi take center stage. These international delicacies, originating from Germany and Korea respectively, represent the diversity and richness of fermented culinary traditions.

Introduction to Fermented Vegetables

Fermented vegetables have a storied history in global cuisines, celebrated not only for their unique flavors but also for their potential health benefits. The process of fermentation involves the breakdown of sugars by microorganisms like bacteria and yeast, transforming raw vegetables into tangy, probiotic-rich creations.

a. Krauts	b. Kimchi
Kraut, the German word for cabbage, forms the foundation of Sauerkraut, a classic fermented cabbage dish. The preparation involves shredding cabbage and layering it with salt in a fermentation vessel. Over time, lactic acid bacteria naturally present on the cabbage initiate the fermentation process, leading to the creation of Sauerkraut. Beyond its distinct flavor, Sauerkraut is prized for its probiotic content, supporting digestive health.	Hailing from Korea, Kimchi is a staple in Korean cuisine and has gained international acclaim for its bold and spicy profile. Kimchi encompasses a wide variety of fermented vegetables, with Napa cabbage being a popular choice. The vegetables are seasoned with a mixture of chili peppers, garlic, ginger, and other spices before undergoing fermentation. Kimchi not only tantalizes the taste buds but also provides a potent dose of probiotics, vitamins, and antioxidants.

Making Krauts and Kimchi at Home

Creating Krauts and Kimchi at home allows for customization and ensures the use of fresh, high-quality ingredients. The basic process involves the following steps:

- **Shredding Vegetables:** For Krauts, cabbage is thinly shredded, while Kimchi may involve various vegetables like Napa cabbage, radishes, and carrots. The goal is to create small, bite-sized pieces that will facilitate the fermentation process.
- **Salting:** Salt is added to the shredded vegetables to draw out moisture. This step not only aids in preserving the vegetables but also creates the ideal environment for beneficial bacteria to thrive. The salted vegetables are left to rest, allowing time for the brine to develop.
- **Spices and Seasonings:** For Krauts, the simplicity lies in the use of cabbage and salt. In contrast, Kimchi embraces a bold array of flavors with the addition of spices like chili flakes, garlic, ginger, and sometimes even fish sauce. The seasoning not only contributes to the taste but also influences the final color and texture of the fermented vegetables.
- **Fermentation:** The seasoned vegetables are packed into jars or fermentation crocks, ensuring that they are fully submerged in their own brine. The containers are then left at room temperature for an extended period, allowing the natural fermentation process to unfold. The duration can vary based on personal preference, with some preferring a shorter fermentation for a milder taste and others opting for a longer fermentation for a more robust flavor.
- **Storing:** Once the desired level of fermentation is achieved, Krauts and Kimchi can be transferred to the refrigerator to slow down the process. This also allows for long-term storage, ensuring a steady supply of fermented vegetables.

Incorporating Fermented Vegetables into Everyday Meals:

The versatile nature of Krauts and Kimchi makes them suitable for a variety of culinary applications. Here's how you can seamlessly incorporate these fermented delights into your everyday meals:

- **Condiment and Side Dish:** Serve Krauts and Kimchi as flavorful condiments or side dishes alongside main courses. Their tangy and spicy notes can complement a range of dishes, adding depth and complexity to the overall dining experience.

- **Sandwiches and Wraps:** Elevate your sandwiches and wraps by incorporating Krauts or Kimchi. The crunchiness and acidity of the fermented vegetables provide a delightful contrast to the other ingredients, creating a harmonious balance of flavors and textures

- **Bowl Toppings:** Enhance your grain bowls or salads by adding a spoonful of Krauts or Kimchi. The probiotic-rich nature of these fermented vegetables not only contributes to gut health but also introduces a burst of flavor to your meal.

- **Stir-Fries and Noodles:** Infuse Krauts or Kimchi into stir-fries or noodle dishes for an extra layer of umami and acidity. The fermented vegetables blend seamlessly with the savory notes of these dishes, offering a unique twist to familiar flavors.

- **Dips and Sauces:** Create zesty dips or sauces by incorporating Krauts or Kimchi. Blending them with yogurt or mayonnaise can result in creamy and flavorful accompaniments for chips, crackers, or vegetable sticks.

Health Benefits of Fermented Vegetables:

The consumption of fermented vegetables, such as Krauts and Kimchi, can contribute to overall health and well-being. Here are some notable health benefits:

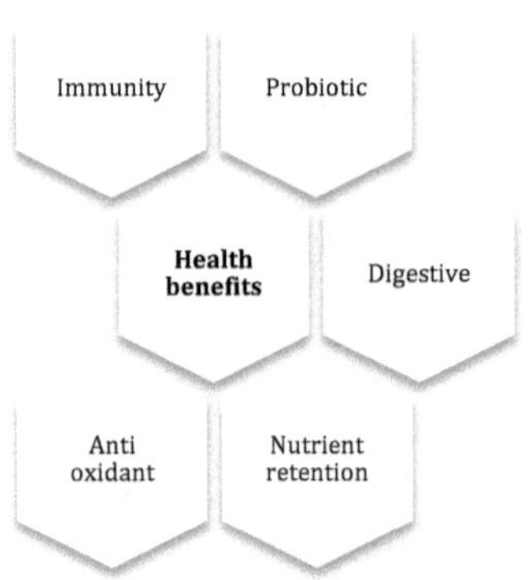

i. **Probiotic Power:** The fermentation process introduces probiotics, which are beneficial bacteria known for their positive impact on gut health. Probiotics play a crucial role in maintaining a balanced and diverse gut microbiome, supporting digestion and immune function.

ii. **Digestive Wellness:** The enzymes produced during the fermentation of vegetables aid in the digestion of nutrients. This can be particularly beneficial for individuals who may experience digestive discomfort, as the enzymes help break down complex compounds into more easily digestible forms.

iii. **Nutrient Retention:** Fermentation preserves and enhances the nutritional content of vegetables. The process can increase the availability of certain vitamins and minerals, making these nutrients more accessible to the body.

iv. **Antioxidant Content:** Fermented vegetables, especially those with vibrant colors like Kimchi, can be rich in antioxidants. These compounds help combat oxidative stress in the body, contributing to overall cellular health.

v. **Immune Support:** The gut plays a significant role in immune function, and a healthy gut microbiome is essential for a robust immune system. The probiotics in fermented vegetables can contribute to immune support by promoting a balanced and resilient gut environment.

In embracing the world of fermented vegetables, we not only indulge our taste buds but also nourish our bodies with a plethora of health benefits. Whether savoring the tanginess of Sauerkraut or the spiciness of Kimchi, the journey into fermented delights is a celebration of flavor, tradition, and well-being. As we incorporate these fermented treasures into our daily meals, we embark on a culinary adventure that transcends borders and embraces the global tapestry of fermented gastronomy.

10. Murabaa: Preserving Tradition, Nourishing Health

In the vibrant tapestry of Indian cuisine, Murabaa stands as a testament to the artistry of preserving fruits through fermentation. Rooted in tradition, Murabaa has been a cherished delicacy for generations, capturing the essence of seasonal fruits in sweet, tangy, and probiotic-rich preserves. In this exploration, we will delve into the intricacies of Murabaa, from its historical significance to diverse recipes and variations. Additionally, we will uncover the health benefits that make Murabaa not only a culinary delight but also a valuable addition to a wholesome diet.

Fermented Fruit Preserves in Indian Cuisine:

The art of fermenting fruits to create Murabaa is deeply embedded in the culinary heritage of India. The process involves harnessing the natural sugars present in fruits to kickstart the fermentation journey. This not only imparts a unique flavor profile to the preserves but also introduces probiotics, making Murabaa a delightful combination of taste and gut-friendly goodness.

Historical Significance:

Murabaa has a rich historical significance, with roots that trace back centuries. In traditional Indian households, the practice of making Murabaa was a way to extend the life of seasonal fruits beyond their harvest periods. The fermentation process not only preserved the fruits but also added depth to their taste, creating a sweet and tangy relish enjoyed throughout the year.

Fermentation Process:

The process of making Murabaa typically involves combining fruits with sugar or jaggery in a controlled environment. The natural sugars in the fruits serve as a substrate for fermentation, inviting the activity of wild yeasts and bacteria. Over time, these microorganisms convert sugars into alcohol and then into acetic acid, giving Murabaa its characteristic sweet and sour taste. The probiotics generated during fermentation contribute to the gut-friendly nature of Murabaa.

Murabaa Recipes and Variations:

The world of Murabaa is diverse, with a plethora of fruits and regional variations contributing to its kaleidoscopic array of flavors. From the iconic Amla (Indian gooseberry) Murabaa to the luscious Mango Murabaa, each variation tells a story of regional preferences and seasonal abundance.

- **Amla Murabaa:** Amla, known for its potent health benefits, is often transformed into Murabaa. The slightly bitter taste of Amla pairs beautifully with the sweetness of sugar or jaggery, creating a unique flavor profile. Amla Murabaa is not only a treat for the taste buds but also a nutritional powerhouse, enriched with vitamin C and antioxidants.

- **Mango Murabaa:** As the mango season unfolds, households across India celebrate by preparing Mango Murabaa. The succulent sweetness of ripe mangoes combines with the tartness of fermentation, resulting in a delectable preserve. Mango Murabaa is not only enjoyed on its own but

Culinary Tradition:

Murabaa has not only been a means of preserving fruits but also a symbol of culinary tradition and hospitality. It is often prepared in larger quantities during the abundant fruit seasons and shared with friends and family. The choice of fruits, the level of sweetness, and the duration of fermentation are often passed down through generations, creating unique family recipes and variations.

is also a versatile ingredient in desserts and culinary creations.

- **Mixed Fruit Murabaa:** Combining an assortment of seasonal fruits, Mixed Fruit Murabaa is a medley of flavors and textures. The variety of fruits introduces complexity, and the fermentation process harmonizes these diverse elements into a cohesive and delightful preserve.

- **Papaya Murabaa:** Papaya, with its tropical sweetness, undergoes a magical transformation in the fermentation process. Papaya Murabaa is known for its distinctive taste and smooth texture, making it a favorite among those who appreciate the nuanced flavors of tropical fruits.

- **Berry Murabaa:** Berries, with their natural sweetness and vibrant hues, lend themselves beautifully to the world of Murabaa. Whether its strawberries, raspberries, or blueberries, the fermentation process enhances the depth of their flavors, creating a Berry Murabaa that is both visually appealing and indulgently delicious.

Health Benefits of Consuming Murabaa

Beyond its exquisite taste, Murabaa brings a host of health benefits to the table, making it a wholesome addition to the diet. The fermentation process not only preserves the nutritional integrity of fruits but also introduces probiotics, contributing to digestive wellness.

i. Probiotic Richness: The fermentation of fruits in Murabaa introduces probiotics, which are beneficial bacteria known for their positive impact on gut health. Probiotics play a crucial role in maintaining a balanced and diverse gut microbiome, supporting digestion and immune function.	**ii. Nutrient Retention:** The fermentation process in Murabaa preserves the natural vitamins, minerals, and antioxidants present in fruits. Unlike traditional preserves that may involve cooking or canning, fermentation allows these nutrients to remain bioavailable, contributing to overall well-being.
iii. Blood Sugar Regulation: The natural sugars present in fruits are broken down during fermentation, potentially leading to a reduction in the overall sugar content of Murabaa. This can be beneficial for individuals looking to manage blood sugar levels while still enjoying a sweet treat.	**iv. Antioxidant Boost:** Fruits, known for their antioxidant content, undergo a concentration of these compounds during the fermentation process. Antioxidants play a crucial role in combating oxidative stress in the body, supporting cellular health and overall vitality.
v. Digestive Wellness: The probiotics in Murabaa contribute to the maintenance of a healthy gut microbiome, which is closely linked to digestive wellness. A balanced and diverse gut microbiome is associated with improved digestion, nutrient absorption, and overall gastrointestinal health.	

11. Fermented "Chutney"

In the diverse landscape of Indian condiments, fermented chutneys emerge as flavorful companions that not only tantalize the taste buds but also contribute to digestive wellness. These traditional condiments, steeped in the art of fermentation, add depth and complexity to meals, creating a symphony of flavors with a probiotic twist. In our exploration of fermented chutneys, we will uncover the essence of their traditional recipes, their role as condiments, and the nuanced flavor profiles that vary across regions.

Traditional Fermented Chutney Recipes

Chutneys, an integral part of Indian cuisine, are often crafted with a diverse array of ingredients ranging from herbs and spices to fruits and vegetables. Fermenting these chutneys adds a layer of depth, allowing the flavors to evolve and mature over time.

- **Mint and Coriander Chutney:** A classic in the world of Indian chutneys, the combination of fresh mint and coriander leaves undergoes fermentation to create a condiment that is both vibrant and aromatic. The probiotics introduced during fermentation enhance the digestive properties of this chutney, making it a staple accompaniment to various dishes.
- **Garlic and Tomato Chutney:** The pungent kick of garlic, combined with the sweetness of ripe tomatoes, results in fermented chutney that is robust and flavorful. The fermentation process softens the sharpness of garlic while introducing probiotics, making this chutney a delightful addition to Indian breads and rice dishes.
- **Coconut and Curry Leaf Chutney:** In South Indian cuisine, coconut-based chutneys are a staple. Fermenting a blend of fresh coconut and curry leaves enhances the umami and complexity of this chutney. The probiotics contribute to its gut-friendly nature, making it a versatile accompaniment for dosas, idlis, and rice dishes.
- **Tamarind and Date Chutney:** The sweet and tangy combination of tamarind and dates undergoes fermentation to create chutney that balances acidity with sweetness. This versatile chutney is often used as a dipping sauce for snacks and chaats, adding a burst of flavor and probiotic goodness.

Using Fermented Chutneys as Condiments

Fermented chutneys play a crucial role in Indian cuisine, serving as condiments that elevate the overall dining experience. Whether paired with snacks, spread on bread, or served alongside main courses, these chutneys contribute a depth of flavor and probiotic richness.

a. Snack Accompaniments: Fermented chutneys, with their bold and nuanced flavors, are ideal companions for Indian snacks. Whether it's samosas, pakoras, or chaats, these chutneys add a zesty and probiotic-rich element, enhancing the overall snacking experience.	**b. Bread Spreads:** Spread on dosas, uttapams, or even sandwiches, fermented chutneys bring a burst of flavor and a probiotic punch. The spreadable consistency of these chutneys allows for easy application, transforming ordinary bread into a delightful culinary experience.

c. **Side Dishes for Rice:** In many Indian households, fermented chutneys are served as side dishes for rice-based meals. The tangy and probiotic-rich nature of these condiments complements the earthy flavors of rice dishes, creating a harmonious balance on the plate.	d. **Dipping Sauces:** Fermented chutneys shine as dipping sauces for a variety of dishes. Whether it's kebabs, grilled meats, or vegetable fritters, the probiotic content adds a dimension of digestive wellness to these savory delights.
e. **Marinades and Dressings:** The versatility of fermented chutneys extends to marinades and dressings. By incorporating these chutneys into marinades for meats or dressings for salads, the probiotics infuse a layer of complexity, enhancing both the flavor and nutritional profile of the dish.	

Flavor Profiles and Regional Differences

One of the enchanting aspects of fermented chutneys is the diversity of flavor profiles that vary across regions in India. Each region boasts its unique combinations of ingredients, spices, and fermentation techniques, resulting in a kaleidoscope of tastes that reflects the culinary traditions of the area.

NEWS Indian chutneys

i. **North Indian Chutneys:** Chutneys in North India often feature bold and aromatic spices such as cumin, coriander, and mustard seeds. The fermentation process deepens these flavors, creating chutneys that are robust, earthy, and well-suited to accompany bread-based dishes like naan and paratha.	ii. **East Indian Chutneys:** Chutneys in East India may showcase the unique flavors of mustard oil and panch phoron, a blend of five spices. The fermentation process melds these distinctive flavors, creating chutneys that are aromatic, slightly pungent, and well-suited to accompany rice and fish dishes.
iii.**West Indian Chutneys:** In the western states of India, chutneys may highlight the freshness of mint, coriander, and jaggery. The fermentation process adds complexity to these chutneys, balancing the sweetness of jaggery with the herbal notes of mint and coriander. They are often served alongside snacks and appetizers.	iv. **South Indian Chutneys:** South Indian chutneys, especially those from Kerala and Tamil Nadu, often incorporate coconut, curry leaves, and tamarind. The fermentation of these chutneys enhances the umami from coconut and introduces a subtle tanginess from tamarind, resulting in condiments that pair beautifully with dosas and rice-based dishes.

Gut Healing Takes Time: Nurturing Your Microbial Ecosystem for Well-Being

In the journey toward digestive wellness, the phrase "Gut Healing Takes Time" encapsulates the understanding that cultivating a healthy and resilient gut is a gradual and ongoing process. Maintaining a healthy gut is not only essential for physical well-being but is increasingly recognized for its impact on mental health and overall vitality. In the quest for gut health, understanding the gradual process of gut healing, recognizing lifestyle factors affecting gut health, and embracing the long-term benefits of a probiotic-rich diet become integral components of fostering a resilient and thriving gut.

Understanding the Gradual Process of Gut Healing

- **Microbial Harmony:** The gut microbiota consists of a diverse array of bacteria, viruses, fungi, and other microorganisms. Achieving and maintaining a balanced and diverse microbial community is vital for gut health. The process of gut healing involves nurturing this harmony and restoring any imbalance that may have occurred due to factors like poor diet, stress, or antibiotic use.

- **The Impact of Diet:** A fundamental aspect of gut healing lies in dietary choices. A diet rich in fiber, prebiotics, and probiotics supports the growth and sustenance of beneficial bacteria in the gut. Fermented foods, such as yogurt, kimchi, and sauerkraut, introduce probiotics, while fiber-rich foods like fruits, vegetables, and whole grains provide nourishment for the gut microbiota.

- **Probiotics and Gut Health:** Probiotics, often referred to as "good" bacteria, play a pivotal role in gut healing. These live microorganisms, commonly found in fermented foods and supplements, have been associated with various health benefits, including improved digestion, enhanced nutrient absorption, and strengthened immune function. Incorporating probiotics into the diet can contribute to the restoration of a healthy microbial balance.

- **Reducing Inflammatory Triggers:** Chronic inflammation can disrupt the delicate balance of the gut microbiota and contribute to gut-related issues. Identifying and addressing inflammatory triggers, such as certain foods or environmental factors, is a key aspect of the gradual process of gut healing. Anti-inflammatory foods, like fatty fish, nuts, and leafy greens, can support this healing journey.

Lifestyle Factors Affecting Gut Health

a. Stress and the Gut-Brain Axis: The gut is intricately connected to the brain through a bidirectional communication system known as the gut-brain axis. Stress, whether acute or chronic, can adversely impact this axis and influence gut health. Mind-body practices such as meditation, deep breathing exercises, and yoga can help mitigate stress and positively affect the gut-brain connection.	**b. Physical Activity:** Regular physical activity has been associated with a diverse and beneficial gut microbiota. Exercise not only promotes overall well-being but also contributes to a healthier microbial composition. Engaging in activities such as walking, jogging, or strength training can positively influence gut health.
c. Sleep Quality: Adequate and quality sleep is crucial for the maintenance of a healthy gut. Disruptions in sleep patterns can alter the gut microbiota and contribute to conditions such as dysbiosis. Establishing a consistent sleep routine and creating a conducive sleep environment are essential for supporting gut health.	**d. Antibiotic Use and Medications:** The use of antibiotics, while often necessary to combat infections, can have a profound impact on the gut microbiota. Antibiotics may unintentionally disrupt the balance of beneficial bacteria. Whenever possible, judicious use of antibiotics and consideration of their potential impact on gut health become important aspects of maintaining a healthy microbial ecosystem.

Long-Term Benefits of a Probiotic-Rich Diet

a. Gut Microbiota Resilience: Consistent consumption of probiotic-rich foods fosters a resilient gut microbiota. A diverse and robust microbial community can better withstand disturbances and recover more effectively from challenges such as infections or dietary changes. This resilience is a key factor in the long-term benefits of a probiotic-rich diet.	**b. Improved Digestive Function:** Probiotics contribute to improved digestive function by enhancing the breakdown and absorption of nutrients. They can also help alleviate symptoms of conditions such as irritable bowel syndrome (IBS) and contribute to overall gastrointestinal comfort.

c. Enhanced Immune Function: The majority of the immune system resides in the gut-associated lymphoid tissue. A well-balanced gut microbiota, supported by probiotics, plays a crucial role in regulating immune responses. A fortified immune system can provide long-term protection against infections and contribute to overall health.	**d. Mood and Mental Health:** Emerging research suggests a strong connection between gut health and mental well-being. Probiotics may positively influence mood and reduce symptoms of anxiety and depression. Long-term adherence to a probiotic-rich diet can contribute to mental resilience and emotional balance.

e. Reduced Risk of Chronic Conditions: A healthy gut microbiota has been linked to a reduced risk of various chronic conditions, including inflammatory bowel diseases, metabolic disorders, and even certain neurological disorders. Long-term commitment to a probiotic-rich diet may contribute to the prevention of these conditions.

In the journey toward gut health, recognizing that "Gut healing takes time" is a foundational principle. It is a gradual process influenced by lifestyle choices, dietary habits, and a consistent commitment to nurturing the symbiotic relationship between the human body and its microbial inhabitants. By understanding the intricate dance of factors that influence gut health, individuals can embark on a path of long-term well-being, where the resilience of the gut microbiota becomes a cornerstone of overall health.

Summary

First section covered the intricate world of the gut microbiome, emphasizing regional diversity in India. It explores the roles of good and bad bacteria, their strains, and their effects on health. The link between gut health and diseases, the impact of microbes on aging, and concepts like gut inflammation, permeability, and autoimmunity are discussed.

Second section focused on common gut issues, this part covers digestion, bloating, and various digestive diseases. It provides insights into FODMAPs, food sensitivities, and microbial imbalances, along with traditional remedies and dietary changes for gut health. Additionally, it addresses the connection between gut health, weight loss, and immune health, emphasizing the importance of the gut-brain axis and hydration

The final section showcased the richness of the Indian diet in promoting gut health through fermented foods. It introduces a variety of probiotic-rich Indian foods, from curd and buttermilk to fermented pickles and chutneys. Emphasizing the slow but effective nature of gut healing, this part encourages the incorporation of these probiotic foods into one's diet for overall well-being.

VINDHYA SINGH

Conclusion

As we navigate the intricate landscape of our bodies, one revelation stands out—the profound influence of our gut microbiome. It's more than a scientific phenomenon; it's a symphony of life within us. This journey through the science of gut microbiome, the challenges we face, and the solutions we discover is a testament to the delicate balance that sustains our well-being. In the diverse tapestry of India, our regional variations extend beyond culture and tradition; they weave into the very fabric of our gut microbiota. The good bugs and bad ones, the silent architects of our health, guide us through the maze of well-being. The revelations of how these microbes impact aging, the nuanced dance of inflammation and permeability, and the profound link to autoimmune conditions underscore the importance of understanding and nurturing our gut.

Yet, in the midst of these complexities, there is hope and wisdom rooted in the heart of Indian cuisine. Our fermented foods, the unsung heroes of gut health, offer a sanctuary for those steering clear of gluten and dairy. From the comforting embrace of curd and buttermilk to the vibrant medley of fermented pickles, pulses, and chutneys, our traditional fare emerges as a beacon of gut-friendly sustenance. In a world marked by dietary challenges, our Indian probiotic-rich diet becomes not just a choice but a celebration of well-being. It's a testament to the age-old wisdom that resides in our kitchens, offering an alternative that transcends the limitations of gluten and dairy. As we embrace these culinary treasures, we embark on a journey of healing—a journey that requires time, patience, and an understanding of the symbiotic dance between our bodies and the foods we consume. So, let's savor the flavors of our heritage, recognizing that in each bite, we nurture not just our bodies but the delicate ecosystem within. The science of gut microbiome becomes a living narrative, and our Indian foods emerge as guardians, guiding us away from the pitfalls of modern dietary challenges. In this emotional ode to our gut, let's celebrate the resilience of our bodies and the timeless wisdom enshrined in the heart of our kitchens.

In the heart of every Indian kitchen, the alchemy of tradition and health intertwines through the artistry of fermented foods. As we savor the tang of pickles, the fluffiness of idlis, and the crispness of dosas, we embark on a journey beyond mere flavors – a journey that touches our very essence. These time-honored creations not only delight our taste buds but whisper tales of well-being. For those days when fatigue clouds our spirit and immunity wavers, the embrace of fermented wonders becomes a comforting balm. In every spoonful, we find a remedy for bloating and a tonic for low energy, and as the probiotics dance within, our gut echoes with gratitude. It's more than just a culinary affair; it's a celebration of vitality. In the radiant tapestry of Indian fermented foods, we discover not just sustenance, but a timeless connection to our health, a reminder that the simplest bites can carry the weight of our well-being. So, let us savor these bites with both gratitude and gusto, for in the folds of fermented traditions, we find a recipe for a healthier, heartier life.

"Nurturing Our Gut, Embracing Indian Wisdom"

References

- Ahmad R, Sorrell MF, Batra SK, Dhawan P, Singh AB. Gut permeability and mucosal inflammation: bad, good or context dependent. Mucosal immunology. 2017 Mar 1;10(2):307-17.

- Belkaid Y, Hand TW. Role of the micro-biota in immunity and inflammation. Cell. 2014 Mar 27;157(1):121-41.

- Bischoff SC, Barbara G, Buurman W, Ockhuizen T, Schulzke JD, Serino M, Tilg H, Watson A, Wells JM. Intestinal permeability–a new target for disease prevention and therapy. BMC gastroenterology. 2014 Dec;14:1-25.

- Clayton JB, Al-Ghalith GA, Long HT, Tuan BV, Cabana F, Huang H, Vangay P, Ward T, Minh VV, Tam NA, Dat NT. Associations between nutrition, gut micro-biome, and health in a novel nonhuman primate model. Scientific reports. 2018 Jul 24;8(1):11159.

- Cryan JF, Dinan TG. Mind-altering microorganisms: the impact of the gut micro-biota on brain and behaviour. Nature reviews neuroscience. 2012 Oct;13(10):701-12.

- Fasano A. Intestinal permeability and its regulation by zonulin: diagnostic and therapeutic implications. Clinical Gastroenterology and Hepatology. 2012 Oct 1;10(10):1096-100.

- Furuta Y, Takahashi K, Shiraki K, Sakamoto K, Smee DF, Barnard DL, Gowen BB, Julander JG, Morrey JD. T-705 (favipiravir) and related compounds: Novel broad-spectrum inhibitors of RNA viral infections. Antiviral research. 2009 Jun 1;82(3):95-102.

- Gewirtz AT, Vijay-Kumar M, Brant SR, Duerr RH, Nicolae DL, Cho JH. Dominant-negative TLR5 polymorphism reduces adaptive immune response to flagellin and negatively associates with Crohn's disease. American Journal of Physiology-Gastrointestinal and Liver Physiology. 2006 Jun;290(6):G1157-63.

- Hills RD, Pontefract BA, Mishcon HR, Black CA, Sutton SC, Theberge CR. Gut micro-biome: profound implications for diet and disease. Nutrients. 2019 Jul;11(7):1613.

- McBurney MI, Davis C, Fraser CM, Schneeman BO, Huttenhower C, Verbeke K, Walter J, Latulippe ME. Establishing what constitutes a healthy human gut micro-biome: state of the science, regulatory considerations, and future directions. The Journal of nutrition. 2019 Nov 1;149(11):1882-95.

- O'Toole PW, Jeffery IB. Gut micro-biota and aging. Science. 2015 Dec 4;350(6265):1214-5.

- Parulekar NN, Kolekar P, Jenkins A, Kleiven S, Utkilen H, Johansen A, Sawant S, Kulkarni-Kale U, Kale M, Sæbø M. Characterization of bacterial community associated with phytoplankton bloom in a eutrophic lake in South Norway using 16S rRNA gene amplicon sequence analysis. PloS one. 2017 Mar 10;12(3):e0173408.

- SINGH A, KUMAR M, GHOSH M, GANGULI A. Traditional Foods and Beverages as Delivery Vehicles for Probiotics. Biotechnology. 2014;8.

- Singh V, Hwang N, Ko G, Tatsuya U. Effects of digested Cheonggukjang on human micro-biota assessed by in vitro fecal fermentation. Journal of Microbiology. 2021 Feb;59:217-27.

- Strober W, Fuss I, Mannon P. The fundamental basis of inflammatory bowel disease. The Journal of clinical investigation. 2007 Mar 1;117(3):514-21.

- Thursby E, Juge N. Introduction to the human gut micro-biota. Biochemical journal. 2017 Jun 1;4/4(11):1823-36.

- Yadav A, Yadav K, Vashistha A. Phosphate solubilizing activity of Pseudomonas fluorescens PSM1 isolated from wheat rhizosphere. Journal of Applied and Natural Science. 2016 Mar 1;8(1):93-6.